THE KALPA SUTRA

AND

NAVA TATVA:

TWO WORKS ILLUSTRATIVE OF THE JAIN RELIGION AND PHILOSOPHY.

TRANSLATED FROM THE MAGADHI.

THE REV. J. STEVENSON, D.D

GYAN

Published by

GYAN

Gyan Publishing House
5, Ansari Road
Daryaganj, New Delhi-110002
Phone: 011-47034999, 9811692060
E-mail: books@gyanbooks.com

Distribution Network

gyanbooks.com

India, USA, Canada, UK, Australia, France

ISBN : 978-81-212-9731-8 (PB)
First Published, 1848

2nd Impression 2023

Printed at: Gyan Press, Delhi.

THE KALPA SUTRA. AND NAVA TATVA
Author: JOHN STEVENSON

THE KALPA SUTRA

AND

NAVA TATVA

Oriental Translation Fund

LONDON.

INSTITUTED 1828.

UNDER THE PATRONAGE OF HIS MOST GRACIOUS MAJESTY

WILLIAM THE FOURTH.

THIS COPY

WAS PRINTED FOR

THE RIGHT HONOURABLE THE

EARL OF SHREWSBURY,

A SUBSCRIBER

TO THE

Oriental Translation Fund.

THE KALPA SUTRA.

AND

NAVA TATVA:

TWO WORKS ILLUSTRATIVE OF THE JAIN RELIGION AND PHILOSOPHY.

TRANSLATED FROM THE MÁGADHI.

WITH

AN APPENDIX,

CONTAINING

REMARKS ON THE LANGUAGE OF THE ORIGINAL.

BY

THE REV. J. STEVENSON, D.D.,

V.P.R.A.S. BOMBAY.

M.DCCC.XLVIII.

TO

LIEUT.-COL. W. H. SYKES, F.R.S., M.R.A.S.,

ETC. ETC.,

THE ZEALOUS PROMOTER

OF

EVERY ENDEAVOUR TO THROW LIGHT ON THE ANTIQUITIES,

OR OPEN UP THE RESOURCES OF INDIA,

A DISTINGUISHED LABOURER IN THE FIELD

OF

ORIENTAL RESEARCH,

THE FOLLOWING WORK IS MOST RESPECTFULLY INSCRIBED,

BY

HIS OBLIGED HUMBLE SERVANT,

J. STEVENSON.

THE FOLLOWING IS A LIST OF THE JAIN TIRTHANKARS, WITH THE COLOURS OF THEIR BODIES AND EMBLEMS.

Name.	Colour.	Emblem.
Rishabha	Yellow	Bull.
Ajita	Ditto	Elephant.
Sambhava	Ditto	Horse.
Abhinandana	Ditto	Ape.
Sumati (a female)	Ditto	Curlew.
Padmaprabha	Red	Red Lotus
Supársva	Yellow	The figure Svastica.
Chandraprabha	White	The Moon or Crescent.
Pushpadanta	Ditto	Crocodile.
Sitala	Yellow	The figure Srívatsa.
Sreyánsa	Ditto	Rhinoceros.
Vásupújya	Red	Buffalo.
Vimala	Yellow	Boar.
Ananta	Ditto	Falcon.
Dharma	Ditto	Spike-headed club.
Sánti	Ditto	Antelope.
Kunthu	Ditto	Goat.
Ara	Ditto	The figure Nandavartta.
Malli	Blue	A Water Jar.
Suvrata	Black	Tortoise.
Nám	Yellow	Blue Lotus.
Nemi	Black	Conch.
Pársva	Blue	Serpent.
Vardhamána	Yellow	Lion.

TRISALA'S DREAMS.

Elephant.	Bull.	Lion-Tiger.	Lakshmí.	A Garland.
Moon.	Sun.	Standard.	Jar.	Lotus Lake.
The Sea.	Heavenly Mansion.	Trisala.	Heap of Pearls.	Flameless Fire.

LUCKY FIGURES.

SRIVATSA.

SATVIKA.

THRONE.

FLOWER-POT.

COUPLE OF FISHES.

MIRROR.

NANDIVARTTA.

VARDHAMÁMA.

TRANSLATOR'S PREFACE.

THE Jains are now well known to the learned in Europe as the only representatives in Hindustan of the adherents to the tenets of Buddhism, a religious community once so numerous in India Proper, and still embracing so many of the inhabitants of the neighbouring countries of Ceylon, Tibet, Burma, China, and its adjacent territories. Without the least disparagement to the learned dissertations that have been published on the Jains, I trust that the following translations, the one, that of their most sacred religious work, and the other, that of their most popular philosophical essay, will not be unacceptable to those who take an interest in the history of the religious opinions and philosophy of India.

Of the eight days in the middle of the rains which are devoted to the reading of those works esteemed peculiarly sacred, no less than five are allotted to the Kalpa Sútra, the first of the works here presented to the English reader. It commences, and is chiefly occupied, with the legendary history of Mahávíra, the last of those deified spiritual legislators, called by the Jains, Tirthankaras. To this are appended the lives of other four sages of the same class, and in some copies those of the whole twenty-four, though it is nearly certain that all of these are by a later hand, and that none except the first, or at any rate the five to whom the precedence is given, are genuine productions of the reputed author. Mahávíra, by the Jains of the Carnatic, is said to have died B.C. 663, by those of Bengal, according to Mr. Colebrooke, in B.C. 637, by those in Gujaráth, in B.C. 527, or as they state it, 470 years before the commencement of the era of Vikrama. Mr. Prinsep in his Useful Tables, Part II., p. 33, makes this event to have happened in B.C. 569, at the age of seventy. This I am inclined to believe is the correct date, not only on account of Mr. Prinsep's great accuracy and tact in all these matters, but also because it agrees best with the statement of the Jains, that Mahávíra was the preceptor of the great Gautama Buddha. The

Ceylonese date of the death of Buddha is B.C. 543, and the death of the Tirthankara having taken place in B.C. 569, we obtain the reasonable period of twenty-six years, for the demise of the preceptor before his pupil. The Kalpa Sútra, according to a date embodied in the work itself, was composed 980 years after the demise of Mahávíra, that is to say, A.D. 411. The public reading of the work took place twelve years afterwards, as narrated in the Introduction. The author's name was Bhadra Báhu, and the sovereign who then reigned in Gujaráth, was Dhruva Sena. The four commentators who, between the fifteenth and seventeenth centuries, have commented on the work, are Yasovijaya, whose Sanskrit work, called Sákhábadha, has been used in making the annexed translation, Devichandra, the Gujaráthi translator chiefly followed, and Jnánavimala, and Sámayasundara.

There is so little of Eastern extravagance exhibited in the age and date of the death of Mahávíra, that one is glad for once to escape exposure to the spirit of scepticism which so generally haunts the European in his antiquarian researches in India, and to grant the author all he demands. The name of the sovereign reigning in Gujaráth at the time, is an important element here, for there are two Dhruva Senas among the Balabhi monarchs, who, at the period above specified, swayed the sceptre in that part of India. The first, indeed, is too early for our purpose, but allowing the second of that name to be in the last year of his reign, as he well might, having lost a grown-up son, then on an average of twenty-one years to him, and his four predecessors, there will be an exact coincidence between our date of the first public reading of the Kalpa Sútra, and that found on the Gujaráth copper-plate grants of the first Sridhava Sena*. In accordance with this early date, the state of civilization described in this work is higher than we have any reason to believe has existed among the Hindus, since the first centuries of our era, and the state of Brahmanical literature, as here depicted, without any mention of the Puráns, tends to the same conclusion. The commentator, indeed, in this latter

---

* Dated Samvat 375, i.e., A.D. 318, i.e., 5 × 21 = 105, which, added to 318, gives 423 = 411 × 12. There is no such name, we may remark, as Dhruva Sena in the modern or restored Balhára dynasty.

point, supplies the omission of the author, and clubs in these modern records of traditions along with the more ancient Itihása, showing the altered state of things when he wrote. I of course take it for granted that the author describes the manners of his own time and place, and not those of the sixth century before our era at Kundagráma and Rájagriha, in Berár, where the scene of his hero's piety and labours is laid. It is a pity the work is so entirely confined to its subject, and that we have none of those historical notices which render the Ceylonese Mahávanso so interesting to Europeans.

I was at first inclined to stop my remarks on the history of the Jain religion at this point, and to concede that through the natural change to which all systems of opinion are liable, it had arisen at the period in question from a corruption of the Buddhistical religion, but a close attention to the list of Theros (*Sans.* Sthírávara) or head teachers from Mahávíra to the author's time, which forms a part of the work, especially the unbrokenness of the chain, and the reasonable number of years assigned to each, has made me hesitate about the correctness of such an assumption. From Mahávíra upwards, indeed, to the preceding Tirthankara Pársvanáth, we have no list of head teachers, but we have only an interval of 250 years, while the term of Párva's sublunary existence is still bounded by the possible number of a hundred years. So far the Jains are reasonable, and measured in their eras, compared with Brahmans and Buddhists; for even the latter throw Sákya's predecessor back to an immense period before the advent of the present Buddha. The moderation of the Jains, up to the time of Pársvanátha, is the more remarkable, as after that they far outstrip all their compeers in the race of absurdity, making the lives of their Tirthankars extend to thousands of years, and interposing between them countless ages, thus enabling us to trace with some confidence the boundary between the historical and the fabulous. There are, however, yet one or two other points in the accounts the Jains give us, which seem to have a historic bearing. The first is the relation said to have subsisted between the last Buddha and the last Tirthankara, the Jains making Mahávíra, Gautama's preceptor, and him the first and favourite pupil of his master. Yet they tell us that not he, but Sridharma, became head of the community after the Tirthankara's death. When pressed for the reason they are silent and mysterious, evidently averse to disclose the fact that he became the founder of a new and rival sect, which for a long time wholly eclipsed their own. Nor are we to look for any hint of this kind in the writings of the Buddhists, as nothing could be said upon the subject without leading to an avowal that the great Sage himself had had an instructor. In favour of the Jain theory, however, it may be noticed, that Buddha is said to have seen twenty-four of his predecessors*, while in the present Kappo he had but four. The Jains, consistently with their theory, make Mahávíra to have seen twenty-three of his predecessors, all that existed before him in the present age. This part of Buddhism then evidently implies the knowledge of the twenty-four Tirthankars of the Jains. Gautama, however, by the force of natural genius, threw their

* Mahávanso, book I., c. i.

system entirely into the shade, till the waning light of Buddhism permitted its fainter radiance to reappear on the Western horizon*.

Mahávíra then, the great hero, as the name implies, of the Jain religion, was a Digambara, and went about in a state of perfect nudity. Pársvanáth, and all his predecessors, if he had any, were clothed in decent apparel, with the single exception of Rishabha, of whom we shall immediately speak· Mahávíra, no doubt, considered the innovation he had made in the established system, a reformation, and necessary to show the perfect sage's entire superiority to all worldly feelings and passions. The common sense of Gautama led him to see that the natural and universal sentiments of mankind cannot be set at nought, or opposed with impunity, and, therefore, he moved about clothed in yellow garments. It was not unlikely, on this very point, that the split took place between him and the other chief men of the Jain community. In modern times, however, the great majority of them

* After writing the above, I found my conclusion anticipated by Mr. Colebrooke, and am happy therefore that it now goes abroad with the suffrage of so learned an Orientalist.—*Trans. R.A.S.*, vol. i., p. 522.

have virtually confessed the superior wisdom of Buddha, by taking a lesson from his institute, and wearing plain white garments, (on which account they are called Svetámbaras), clothing themselves without servilely copying the yellow robes of the Buddhist priesthood, leaving such mimicry to Hindu Bairágís and Gosains, sectaries who endeavour to combine the Buddhistical monkery with the Brahmanical theology. The revival of the Digambara practice is said by the other party to have taken place through the efforts of Sahasra Mallika, about a century before the commencement of our era, since which time the sects have kept entirely separate from one another. It is much more likely however, from what is said above, that the Svetámbara party originated about that time, and not the Digambara.

The second point in the Jain traditions which I imagine has a historical basis, is the account they give of the religious practice of Rishabha, the first of their Tirthankars. He, too, like Mahávíra, is said to have been a Digambara. In the Brahmanical Puranic records, he is placed second on the list of kings, in one of the regal families, and said to have been father to that Bharat from whom India took its name. He is also said, in the end of his life, to have abandoned the world, going about everywhere as a naked ascetic. It is so seldom that Jains and Brahmans agree, that I do not see how we can refuse them credit in this instance where they do so, the only point of difference between the two parties being, that while the Jains maintain that Rishabha followed an institute worthy of being adopted by sages in every age, the Brahmans stoutly maintain that no one is authorized to follow his example. However this may be, it is certain that even according to the traditions preserved by the Bráhmans themselves, Rishabha, Kapila, Gautama, and other sages, maintained opinions, and followed practices, which vary much from the present orthodox standard, and if in these early ages there was no regular Jain or Buddhistical organization, as little was there an exclusive Brahmanism. The truth seems to be, that at the period referred to there was no regular division of caste among the people, of schools among the philosophers, nor of sects among religionists. All shades of opinion and practice were tolerated; the broachers of new theories, and the introducers of new rites did not revile the established religion, and the adherents of the old Vedic system of elemental worship looked on the new notions as speculations they could not comprehend, and the new austerities as the exercise of a self-denial they could not reach, rather than as the introduction of heresy and schism. And such, it may be remarked in passing, is the very view taken of the opinions and practices of Bairágís and Gosáins by nine-tenths of the Hindus of the present day. After a time, however, either sectarian zeal became too strong for its possessors to abstain from taunting the followers of the old system with their obtuseness, or the others, alarmed at the prevalence of these novelties, ran with fire and sword to the rescue of the old superstitions, and thus a schism was perpetrated, which, at one particular era at least, that in which Buddhism fell and the modern Saiva system of Hinduism was established, made India a field of contention to opposing religious sects, and with the extermination of that religion which had been dominant during the period of its greatest glory, occasioned the loss of those historical documents, which recorded the largesses and exploits of the sovereigns of a hostile faith. During the early ages, the religious warfare in India was carried on, as far as we can learn, chiefly by the legitimate weapons of discussion and argument, though the edicts of Asoka, no doubt, had arguments founded on the logic of the Emperor, as well as on that of the Dialectician. The open practice of sacrifice, and other Brahmanical rites, was prohibited; but there was no reason for supposing that, while the Buddhists had the superiority, they ever so far contradicted the precepts of their religion as to shed the blood of their fellow creatures in a holy war. The same cannot be said of the Brahmans, who themselves admit that, under the direction of Kumarilla Bhatta, about the eighth century of our era, carnal weapons were employed to put down the Buddhistical and exalt the Saiva faith.

The last division of the Kalpa Sútra is a digest of monkish rules, to guide the sages during the Paryúshana, or Lenten period, a section of the book which requires no remark. It may be useful, however, to exhibit in a few articles the Jain belief, on those points which to a European (though not always to an Indian) seem of first importance.

1. The Jains then believe that the world, consisting of intellectual as well as material principles, has existed from all eternity, undergoing an infinite number of revolutions, produced simply by the inherent physical and intellectual powers of nature, without the intervention of any eternal Deity, no such Being, distinct from the world, having any existence, though certain of the world's elements, when properly developed, obtain deification.

2. That in every great cycle of years twenty-four Tirthankars are manifested in the Bharat Khanda of Jambu Dvípa, our India. These are not only Sádhus, rising from manhood to deity, by the force of meditation, but are also Divine Legislators, each laying down a particular institute for the purification of mankind: whence they derive their name*. Though at present there are no Tirthankars in India, in other terrestrial districts there are no less than twenty.

* यस्तीर्थं करोति स तीर्थङ्करः The Jain Tirtha is a moral one.

3. That the country of Bharat, our India, and an equal portion on the other side of the globe called Airavartta, are alone subject to a depopulating catastrophe at the end of a great cycle of years. The rest of the terrestrial circle, either inhabited by Mlechchhas, Barbarians, or by Yugalas, hermaphrodites not exposed to toil, or the subjects of virtue and vice, remains unchanged.

4. That shortly after the desolation of the abode of man, above mentioned, colonies of Yugalas came from their own proper continent to repeople the waste territories, and from change of situation and manner of living become men, and give rise to a new race of human beings. The Jains, however, leave unexplained how these Yugalas began to exist, and hide themselves amid the darkness of their prime absurdity—an infinite succession of finite beings.

5. They maintain, like the Brahmans, that there is a number of heavens and hells, for temporary rewards and punishments. The gods whom they allow to possess several of these heavens are but beings, who were once men or animals, enjoying the reward of inferior kinds of merit, and who must

descend again to earth, and be born anew, and continue ever in the whirl of transmigrations, unless they become sages. The chief of these gods is named Sakra, or in Mágadhi, Sakke, the Sakko of the Buddhists, and the Indra of the Brahmans. The modern Jains have made of the one, sixty-four Sakras, and surname the lord of heaven, Sudharma.

6. The sage, who by meditation frees his mind from all worldly attachments, obtains at death Nirvána, a state of perfect bliss, perfect knowledge, and freedom from all pain and mutation, ascends to the highest heavens, called Siddha Silá (the Rock of the Perfect), and exalted far above the gods, becomes a special object of adoration to gods and men.

7. The Jain community consists of two great sections, somewhat analogous to our clergy and laity, each section embracing both males and females. The clerical males are named Sádhus, *i. e.*, Sages. All profess celibacy, live in monasteries or houses, in communities of from four or five to a hundred, in subjection to an abbot, and perform all the priestly acts of the Jain religion. The Sadhwinis, or Nuns, live also in separate communities,

but these now are very few in number. The Jain laity are called Srávakas, *i.e.*, Hearers; the females being termed properly Srávakís. They have among them a modified form of caste; and what wonder, since in Southern India Mohammedans and Christians have the same? They practise also a number of aboriginal and Brahmanical superstitions, at which the priesthood wink, though they disapprove of them.

8. The practical part of the Jain religion consists in the performance of five duties, and the avoidance of five sins. The duties are, 1st, mercy to all animated beings; 2nd, almsgiving; 3rd, venerating the sages while living, and worshipping their images when deceased; 4th, confession of faults; 5th, religious fasting. The sins are, 1st, killing; 2nd, lying; 3rd, stealing; 4th, adultery; 5th, worldly-mindedness.

9. A striking feature of the Jain religion is, the keeping of the season of religious meditation, reading, and fasting, called the Paryúshana, or, popularly, Pajjúsan. It corresponds to the Buddhist Wasso, and is divided into two parts, the fifty days that precede, and the seventy that succeed

the fifth of Bhádra, Sukla Paksha. The Svetámbaras fast during the former period, and the Digambaras during the latter. The Paryúshana this year (1847) will commence about the 26th of July, but by the neglect of the precession of the equinoxes it is too late by three weeks, like all other Hindu festivals that have reference to the solar revolution, and therefore does not so well correspond to the four months of the rainy season in Gujarath and Upper India as it otherwise would have done.

10. The last thing I shall advert to is the existence among the Jains of the confessional, and the necessity that exists of confessing at least once a year to a priest, and obtaining from him ghostly absolution. Burdened consciences confess at all times, and have various kinds of fasts imposed on them as penances. It is, however, only at the commencement of the holy season that it is considered imperative upon every good Jain to confess to a priest. I must own that I was at first a little startled at the discovery of this article in the Jain creed, and thought I must have made some mistake in interpreting the word Padikaman

(*Sans.* Pratikramaña), by which term the duty is technically expressed; but abundant oral and written explanations, as well as the context of several passages where the word occurs, have removed every doubt. The Gujarathi word that expresses the priestly absolution, is Álavan. Although the rite of confession does not, as far as I can learn, exist among the Buddhists, it most likely had its origin in India in an early age, and along with other opinions and practices, travelled westward in the early centuries of Christianity, and obtained incorporation with a purer faith.

For an account of the Jain uranography and geography, I must refer the reader to the *Asiatic Researches,* vol. ix. Their system seems to have been formed before that of the Brahmans, as they have but three terrestrial continents and two seas. It contains, however, numberless absurdities, and has not the slightest title to the name of science. An arc of a circle, whose diameter is a hundred thousand yojanas, is made to represent the coast of India from the Ganges to the Indus, shewing an utter ignorance of the existence even of the Peninsula. No wonder Ptolemy erred, when natives blundered so egregiously. The same absurdity is embodied in the system of the Brahmans. A word of explanation is required relative to the two Jain cycles, called Avasarpini and Utsarpini, whose lengths are exactly the same. The reader is to fancy a serpent in infinite space, coiled up, so that the tail shall touch the head. The earth is now moving down this serpent from the head to the tail, therefore this is an Avasarpini (going down the serpent). When it arrives at the extremity of the tail it cannot go on, but must return, and its progress upwards is called an Utsarpini (going up the serpent). Each of these periods is divided into six aras or eras, comprehending ten crores (100,000,000) of sagaras of years. A sagara or ocean of years, my Jain informant assures me, (though Mr. Colebrooke's explanation of this knotty point is a little different), is the number of the small points of the excessively fine hair of Yugalas, which a pit of the dimensions of a cubic yojana would contain, the hairs being so closely packed together that a river of water running over them would not dislodge one of them.

In the prefixed scheme of the emblems of the

different Tirthankars, it may strike the reader that there is no vestige of anything like the Buddhist Chaitya in any of them. This arises from one remarkable feature of dissimilarity between the Jains and Buddhists. The Dagoba, or Buddhist Chaitya, was a place originally appropriated to the preservation of relics, a practice as abhorrent to the feelings of the Jains as it is to those of the Brahmans. The word Chaitya, when used by the Jains, means any image or temple dedicated to the memory of a Tirthankar.

The Philosophical Tract at the end of the book, as well as the Kalpa Sútra, has already been analyzed by Mr. Colebrooke, yet I trust the learned reader will be glad also to see it entire. I have enjoyed advantages in the study of the Jain literature on this side of India, which are unattainable in Bengal; yet, wherever I have had occasion to differ in the sense of any passage from that learned Orientalist, the reader may rest assured that I have first of all well weighed the comments of the Annotator, as well as carefully studied the context, before I have come to a decision. The Jains, while well acquainted with, and frequently referring to, the Sánkhya, Nyáya, Chárváka, and Vaishesika systems of Hindu philosophy, do not acknowledge the Vedánta. This is one of several reasons which makes me suspect that the whole of the Upanishads, as well as the Puráns, have been composed since the fall of Buddhism, the latter, no doubt, to fill up the blank left in history by the destruction or neglect of Buddhist works, and the former to fill up a similar chasm in the systems of philosophy.

I have considered it expedient to write the proper names and technical terms, generally according to the Sanskrit form, rather than according to the original orthography. The modern Jains themselves have substituted the Sanskrit for the Mágadhi in their religious writings, and the sight of an ugly mark of interrogation, stuck to the end of such a word as Pajúshan, even in the *Transactions of the Royal Asiatic Society*, would have scared a stouter heart than mine from the use of the Mágadhi orthography. On the nature of the language itself, and the form it assumes in the Jain literature, some remarks are made in the Appendix.

With all the attention I have been able to bestow, and the care I have exercised to avoid error, I am not sanguine enough to suppose that future inquirers will not detect blemishes and mistakes in my translation and remarks; yet, if I shall have succeeded in any degree in throwing light on the workings of the human mind, and on the history of a sect interesting in itself, but especially so in its relation to Buddhism, I shall not consider my labour lost.

KALPA SÚTRA.

INTRODUCTION.

Em. Om.* *Adoration to the propitious Pársvanátha.*

Having prostrated myself before the glorious Mahávíra, and brought before the mind Gautama, the Religious Instructor, I proceed to expound the Kalpa Sútra in the comment called the Kalpalatá.

Religion is the vital principle† of the world,

---

* Em means the female energy or cause of the world, and Om the male, answering to our material and efficient causes. This line is merely prefixed by the scribe, and does not belong to the work.

† I have rendered सार by these two phrases, as the best I could think of.

The whole sentence which holds here so important a place is as follows :—

धर्म्मो जगतस्सारः। सर्वसुखानां प्रधानहेतुत्वात्।
तस्योत्पत्तिर्मनुजाः। सारं तेनैव मानुष्ये॥

since it is the first cause of all felicity. It proceeds from man, and it is by it also that man attains the chief good*. From religion, birth in a good family is obtained, bodily health, good fortune, long life, and prowess. From religion also spring pure renown, a thirst for knowledge, and increase of wealth. From the darkest gloom, and every dreaded ill, religion will ever prove a saviour. Religion when duly practised bestows heaven, and final emancipation†.

The sages who, maintaining the regular succession of spiritual authority, sit four months yearly at Anandapura‡, the sacred place appointed by our ancient Teachers, for the purpose of reading to the select congregated multitude our religious books, read also to obtain merit, for five days and nine kshañas, before a public assembly the propitious Kalpa Sútra§.

Kalpa here means the religious practice of the Sages‖; and in it there are ten varieties: 1st,

---

* *Vide* preceding note.

† स्वर्गापवर्गप्रद:

‡ This city is now called in Gujaráthi, Bádnagar.

§ The former of these two assemblies is composed of the priesthood alone. The reason of the difference is given further on.

‖ साधूनां आचार:

Achelakka; 2nd, Udesía; 3rd, Siyyáyara; 4th, Ráyapitha; 5th, Kiíkamme; 6th, Vaya; 7th, Jetha; 8th, Padikamaňe; 9th, Másam; 10th, Pajjosavaña*.

1. What, then, is meant by Achelakka? He who is without *chela,* that is to say, clothing, is Achelaka, and the abstract noun formed from that it is Achailakya† (unclothedness). Achailakya is the attribute of Ṛishabha and Mahávíra‡ alone of all the principal Yatis, they having no other clothing than some covering of old white cloth. Ajita and the rest of the twenty-two Tirthankars being dressed in clothes, valuable and of a variety of colours, though still with holy dispositions, are said to be in the state of Suchelakatwa (well-clothedness). Whether any one else who dresses in coarse white clothes may be considered as in the state of Achailakya is not determined. To those then belongs especially the first Kalpa.

---

* The original Mágadhi words are as follows :—

अचेलक्क उडेसीअ सिय्यायर रायपिठ किईकम्मे
वय जेठ पडिकमणे मासं पज्जोसवण कप्पे

The Sanskrit equivalents will soon appear in their proper places in the text.

† This is now the Sanskrit form introduced by the author, and continued during the whole paragraph, to the exclusion of the Mágadhi.

‡ That is to say, the first and last Tirthankars.

2. The second Kalpa is the Uddesíka, or the accepting of necessaries without asking for them; since such is the meaning of the word. It is an institute intended for sages. Rice with split pulse, water, sweetmeats, betel leaf with betel-nut, clothing, vessels, a house and necessary furniture, may be received by such. This institute belongs to the first and last of the Tirthankars. It may have reference to one, or to a company, or to a whole college of sages. It is not applicable to all the sages. To the twenty-two Tirthankars, and others who enjoy a superior regimen, it is inapplicable; to the rest, however, it applies.

3. The Sidhyátara Kalpa* has reference to a householder. To him belongs a superior regimen to that above mentioned; viz., bread with rice and pulse†, water, sweetmeats, betel-nut and leaf, clothes, vessels, blankets, a broom, a needle, pincers, a nail-parer, and ear-cleaner, these twelve different articles. This institute is not applicable to the whole of the Jina Tirthankar Sages. Further, when there is a want of proper food in the place where a sage resides, or difficulty in procur-

* In the Maráthi language, सिधा means prepared but uncooked victuals, as cleaned rice, &c.

† The original here is अशन the same as above. The difference of translation is owing to a difference in the comment.

ing a residence, or danger of falling into sin*, the Sidhyátara may take from a disciple receiving religious instructions, and freely giving them, grass, hardened earth†, ashes, an earthen pan‡, a high stool, a low stool, a couch, bedding, ointment, and so forth.

4. The fourth Kalpa is the Rájapiñda, or royal establishment. Its constituent parts are—a commander-in-chief, a chief priest, a chief banker§, a prime cabinet minister, a master of the chariots, and, together with the protection of the realm, the before-mentioned twelve articles of regimen. These things then belong only to an anointed king, and hence do not accord with the religious practice of the first and last Tirthankars. But the Rájapiñda was possessed by the other twenty-two, at the same time that there was no imperfection in their wisdom, and they were free from all sin.

---

* The thing chiefly contemplated by Yatis here is the prevalence of insects, and the consequent danger of committing sin by treading on them.

† Probably bricks hardened in the sun, so commonly used in India for building.

‡ To be used as a pot de chambre.

§ A kind of Rothschild, to supply the sovereign with funds on emergencies. He is called here श्रेष्ठी (whence the Gujarathi, Set,) and holds to the State a relation somewhat like that of the Governor of the Bank of England.

5. The fifth Kalpa is Kritíkarma. It consists of two parts; first, the rising and standing upright; and next, the performing of the twelve forms of salutation. This was incumbent upon all the Tirthankars, as well as on other sages, and is to be performed by all to all mutually in the order of their initiation—the newly initiated sage is to be saluted with religious reverence, even by those who have been the longest time initiated; for it is religion that gives man pre-eminence*.

6. The sixth is the Vrĭta Kalpa. Vrĭta here means the highest kind of religious observances. These, in reference to the twenty-two Jina Sages, are four, since they are permitted to marry. But from the absence of all defect in wisdom, to the first and last Jina Sages they are five†.

7. The seventh is called the Jyeshtha Kalpa. Here Jyeshtha means the chief or initiatory rite, and it is to this, as the commencement of a series of observances, that the Institute applies. The performance of the initiatory rite by the first and last Jinas, is to be counted from the time they

---

* पुरुषप्रधानत्वात् धर्मस्य So are the words which I translate as above; the last word in another copy is omitted, and the meaning seems simply to be, that all sages are rendered equal by the possession of the religious character.

† These four principal virtues are the following:—Dána, Síla, Japa, Bháva. See Part I., Book I, chap. 8.

performed the Sámáyaka Charitra, and in relation to the intermediate Yatis, from the day of their performing the Atichára Charitra.

8. The eighth is called the Pratikramaña Kalpa. The Atichára ceremony might be performed or not by Saint Rĭshabha and Maháví́ra, but the Pratikramaña (going to confess to a spiritual guide) they were required to perform twice. On other munis the Pratikramańa is imperative whenever they commit a fault,—otherwise it is not required.

9. The ninth is the Másakalpa. The Másakalpa, which is limited to the first and last Jinas, requires that no one stay longer at a place than a month. This was not imperative on the intermediate Jinas. On the contrary, some of them stayed in the same place for ten millions of years. The Institute does not require any one to stay in the same place for a month; if he have a proper reason, he may leave during its currency.

10. The tenth is the Paryúshana Kalpa. By Paryúshana is meant the religious session of the Sages during the rains. This is a yearly festival, and it is positively enjoined that such a session of the Assembly of Sages should commence on the fifth day after the new moon of Bhádrapad*.

---

* We have here several rather trivial anecdotes introduced,

I now proceed to mention the qualities of the place where the Institute of the Parúyshana is to be performed. The Sages remain seventy days in the same place, unless there be a good reason for removing. Proper reasons for so doing are the following: Not being able to find a proper place to sleep on; the difficulty of procuring provisions; the occurrence of any disaster; the fear of hostile sovereigns, disease, or bodily pain. In such cases it is lawful to remove to another place. A place is unfit, if it swarm with insects, if it be otherwise unclean, if there one is kept in dread of musquitoes, fire, or serpents. In such cases it is proper to remove. Again, the Sages should remain after the four months are completed, if the rains continue so as to make the roads impassable on account of the mud. Then only, however, should the Sages remain beyond the month of Kártik. Places suitable for carrying on the religious exercises of the season are places where there is not much mud, where there are not many creeping insects, where there are no impurities, at a distance from women, where the produce of the cow abounds, where the body of the people is large and respectable, where there are good physicians and medi-

---

to shew the benefit of different forms of religious practice, all tending to prove that different dispositions require different treatment.

cines easily procurable, where there are the habitations of householders who are living with their families, where cattle and grain are abundant, where the king is a just ruler, where the Brahmans and those of their party do not treat our Munis with contempt, where food is easily procured, where reading of the sacred books can be purely performed, and where there is open and level ground to walk about. Such a place, then, is to be esteemed favourable, and there the festival of the sacred rest is to be performed*. When, then, the Sages are met to keep the Parúyshana, this Kalpa Sútra is to be read for the attainment of merit during five days. This Institute is like Indra among the gods, the Moon among the heavenly bodies, Ráma among just rulers, Kámadeva among well-proportioned men, Rambhá among beautiful women, Bhambha among musicians, Airávat among elephants, Rávaña among daring adventurers, Abhaya among wise men, Satrunjaya among holy places†, humility among virtuous qualities, gold among metals, the nine-lettered among charms ‡, the strawberry mango-tree among trees, Sitá among faithful wives, the Gita

---

* Here again an illustrative anecdote is omitted.

† This is a Tirtha of the Jains, thirty-four miles from Bhownagur, in Guzarath.

‡ Probably Sríman Mahávíráya Namah.

among inspired writings, musk among perfumes, gold sand* among articles of commerce, the peacock among dancers†, the five-marked colt‡ among horses, the water of immortality among liquids, melted butter among gravies, the dutiful son Salabhadra among enjoyments, Sántináth among the givers of gifts, Nemináth among chaste religious students, Nandana among forests, the Chandana among woods, friendship among virtues, and the Jain religion among religions. In fine, the Kalpa Sútra is the gem in the crown of all religious institutes. There is no god superior to the Arhat (Jain sage§), no future bliss superior to Mukti (liberation), no holy place superior to Sri Satrunjaya, and no inspired book superior to the Sri Kalpa Sútra. This Kalpa is an ever-present Kalpa Druma (tree yielding whatever is desired), since, to speak of its several parts, the Srí Víra Charitra is the seed, the Sri Párswa Charitra is the sprout, the Sri Nemi Charitra is the stem, the Sri Rishabha Charitra is the branchy top, Sthavirávali

---

* तेजमतुरी is the original, a word I neither ever heard or saw elsewhere.

† नृत्येषु *i. e.* those who strut about in a theatre.

‡ A white horse with black feet and face, or a brown or black horse with white feet and face.

§ The original here is important, and I therefore give it:—

नार्हतः परमोदेवो न मुक्तेः परमं पदं

is the blossoms, the knowledge of the Samáchári is the scent, and the obtaining of liberation is the fruit. And why should I add more? since from reading or giving aid at the lecture, or from listening to all the letters of this Kalpa, along with the proper reverential ceremonies, emancipation is obtained after the eighth transmigration, according to the following text: "O Gautama, they who hear twenty-one times with an attentive mind the Institute of the Jain Religion, performing the proper reverence, and bringing the proper gifts to the venerable sages, are saved from this world's abyss." This treatise, then, is to be read on the fifth day after the new moon of Bhádrapad, according to our Institutions. Among the Digambara community, it is read during the eight days of the great festival of Jamáli, when they continue fasting, and make the figure of Nandidrípa under the name of Yasodhara Charitra. It forms also part of the Institute for the Rĭshi Panchamí, the origin of which I now relate*. There was a certain Brahman in the city of Pushpavati, whose father and mother were dead. In process of time they

* As this is one of the best of our author's stories, and tends to show in what light the Jains view Brahmanism, I have given it a place in the text. It is indeed a severe satire on those who entertain their friends from the proceeds of oppression, exercised towards their inferiors and the brute creation.

were born anew in this their son's house, the former as a bull, and the latter as a bitch. By and bye also, the day of the festival for the *manes* came round. On it the son hired out the bullock to an oilman to labour at his oil-press, and having procured a sufficient quantity of milk, prepared rice and milk for the dinner of those Brahmans who came to the festival. At that juncture the bitch, in which was the soul of his mother, by a certain wonderful knowledge, saw the poison of a snake fall into the rice and milk*, and knowing it would be the cause of great misfortune, went and took it out with her mouth. The Brahman flew at her in a passion, and almost broke her back for her pains, and went and tied her up in the cow-house, and afterwards prepared more rice and milk, and feasted his Brahman guests. In the evening the oilman bound up the bull in the cow-house, without giving him an article to eat or drink after his day's toil. There, looking at the suffering bitch, the bullock exclaimed, "What have I suffered to-day through this sinful son of mine!" The bitch then also began to tell about the pain in her back; when the son, who was lying down at no great distance, overheard their discourse, and understood that these were his father and mother.

---

* चीर in the original, a common dish on festive occasions.

Immediately he got up, and fed them with the remains of the rice and milk, and, leaving home, went to the Rishis*, to inquire how his father and mother could be liberated from their present state. They, after informing him that the reason of their having been born in these bestial forms, was their having devoted themselves to pleasure at improper seasons, commanded him, in order to obtain their liberation, to eat nothing procured by labour on that fifth day of the month. He followed their directions, and the holiday afterwards became celebrated among the people as the Rishi Panchamí.

I am now to mention the author of the Kalpa Sútra. He was Sri Bhadra Báhu Svámi, an accomplished scholar, who was well acquainted with the fourteen branches of his subject†, and a distinguished teacher. Taking for his guide the works here named—the Daśaśrutaskandha, Ashtamádhyáyana, and the discourse called Pratyákhyána, in which he found nine branches—he composed the Kalpa Sútra. He wrote the first

---

* This is the name given to the images of the Buddhist Sages at Ellora, Karli, &c., not by Jains only, but by Hindus and Brahmans. It was to Jain Sages, then, that this Brahman went, and was by them taught to change the most imperative feast of his religion into a fast.

† In the original पूर्व

branch with a solid piece of ink as large as an elephant, the second with a piece as large as two elephants, the third with one the size of eight, the fifth of sixteen, the sixth of thirty-two, the seventh of sixty-four, the eighth of one hundred and twenty-eight, the ninth of two hundred and fifty-six, the tenth of five hundred and twelve, the eleventh of one thousand and twenty-four, the twelfth of two thousand and forty-eight, the thirteenth of four thousand and ninety-six, the fourteenth of eight thousand one hundred and ninety-two. So that the whole was written with sixteen thousand three hundred and eighty-three pieces of ink, each the size of an elephant*; and is therefore called the Mahápurush (the great male)†. Its essence is most profound; and therefore, though a man had a thousand tongues in one mouth, and in one breast perfect knowledge, still he would be unable duly to celebrate the majesty of the Kalpa Sútra.

On the evening of the fifth day of the new moon of Bhádrapad, the reading of the sections of the Kalpa Sútra commenced. It was read, after mak-

---

* This ridiculous story, with its geometrical progression, will serve to initiate the reader a little into the extravagant system of modern Jain exaggeration.

† This is a Brahmanical word for the Deity, and on that account here used.

ing confession, by some one appointed for the purpose, while all the rest of the sages sat in the attitude of devout listeners*. This was the ancient practice, but it has been superseded by a somewhat different ritual since the nine hundred and eightieth year of the era of Mahávíra†. At that time, at Anandapura, now called Bádnagar, lived King Dhruvasena‡. He had a dearly beloved son named Senágaja, who by divine decree died that year at the commencement of the Paryúshana. The king was overwhelmed with grief, and no more came to the place where the Sages lived to pay his respects; and, according to the saying, "As is the king so are the subjects§," the bankers and merchants, and others, failed in their attendance, and occasioned great detriment to religion. Perceiving this, the Religious Director went to the King Dhruvasena, and said, "O king, through your indulgence in grief the whole city and all the country around is overwhelmed with sorrow. Remember, however, O king, that life is fleeting, and the world insipid. It is not proper for a king like you, instructed in the Jain religion, to indulge any

* The original is कायोत्सर्ग a technical word among the Jains.

† B. C. 453 or 411. See Preface.

‡ See Preface. This city is probably the same as Balabhi.

§ यथा राजा तथा प्रजाः

more in grief. We are at present going on with the religious Institute called the Kalpa Sútra, which produces much profit to the hearers by breaking the bonds of action*. If your majesty will come to the place of the religious meeting, it is in the course of being read." The king consented, and the whole was read before him and his followers at nine sittings†, while at the same time they brought presents to the Sages. Ever after this the custom prevailed of reading the Kalpa Sútra before the people generally; and therefore, according to former practice, I read it to you. It is an Institute venerated by Sura (gods), Seura (demons), by men and women; and whosoever three times listens to it, performing also the religious duties that are suitable to the occasion, obtains the highest bliss. The meanings of the Kalpa Sútra are infinite, as numerous as the grains of sand on the brink of all the rivers on the earth, or the drops of water in the sea. How then can one of limited intelligence, like me, explain them? Nevertheless, incapable as I am, I shall make at

---

* कर्मचयकारकं

† Five days were occupied morning and evening in reading the original and hearing its exposition. Formerly the first day seems to have been a broken day, an evening lesson only being read. Now the time is filled up by reading at the last sitting all the original a second time, without comment.

least the attempt to read the Institute before this propitious assembly.

The five following duties are those, which, without fail, must be performed during the reading of the work. The reverencing of the images of deified saints—venerating the Sages—the yearly confession—mutual forgiveness of faults—the right kind of austerity (*i.e.* fasting one whole day, and eating but one meal on the preceding and succeeding day)*. Besides these, the following religious acts are incumbent upon the Srávakas†. The writing of the Kalpa Sútra, text and comment, which is a special duty, since the hearing alone may become the means of liberation after the third transmigration. They should perform the fasts as far as their ability permits. Everywhere in the city proclamation is to be made by sound of trumpet, forbidding to kill any living creature‡.

---

* चैत्यपरिपाठो समस्तसाधुवंदनं सांवत्सरिकप्रतिक्रमणं मिथ: साधर्मिकं ग्रमणं अष्टमंतपस्य

† Auditors, *i. e.* the Jain laity.

‡ This is called the अमारीघोषनाद्. Asoka's famous edicts seem to have been such a proclamation committed to writing, and engraved on stone to render them more permanent. From this and other places it appears that on the Jain laity the following five duties are at all times incumbent:—Mercy to all living creatures, the giving of gifts, the cherishing of pious

Gifts are also to be made in a proper vessel, such as betel-nut, cocoa-nuts, and so forth; pious dispositions are to be cherished; all worldly plans for the time abandoned; the images of those divine beings who have overcome the passions are to be worshipped, and the auspicious Assembly of Sages venerated. The body is to be placed in a devotional position for the destruction of works. Continence also is to be preserved; all show and parade are to be rejected, and money expended according to every one's means, and a religious festival observed. The book of the Kalpa Sútra should then be presented with religious reverence, that is to say, after having brought the book into the house, and the people there having continued watching all night, in the morning, having called the inhabitants of the city, and having cast on them saffron powder, and given them betel-nut, the book is to be put into the hands of a youth mounted on an elephant. The whole multitude are now to accompany it with music and singing, and to place it in the hands of the spiritual guide, for the purpose of being read, while a suitable present to procure necessaries for the reader is also to be made. He who presents the volume of the Kalpa Sútra with all these ceremonies, and com-

---

dispositions, worship of the images of the Tirthankars, and veneration and support of the priesthood.

plete in all its letters, listening also to it when read, obtains emancipation at least after the eighth transmigration*.

The Kalpa Sútra has three subjects:—The history of the first and last Jina; the Sthirávali (list of sages); and the Samáchári (rules of conduct).

---

* The story of Nágaketu, who, in virtue of these ceremonies, revived after being seemingly dead, is here told before the commencement of the Sútras; but as it adds nothing to the information previously given, I have not thought it necessary to insert it.

THE KALPA SÚTRA.

BOOK I.

THE LIFE OF MAHÁVÍRA*.

CHAPTER I.

HIS INCARNATION.

Adoration to the sages who have risen to be worthy of divine honour. Adoration to those who have attained perfection. Adoration to those who regulate our religious services. Adoration to our spiritual

* The proper name of the last Tirthankar is Vardhamána, but both in this work and in common usage the above epithet, meaning the Hero, has so completely usurped the place of the other, that it would be affectation to make the required substitution in the translation.

*instructors. Adoration to the sages in every part of the world**.

Such is the fivefold adoration, the destroyer of all sin, and of all bringers of good fortune, the most fortunate.

The venerable ascetic Mahávíra, in the age and time of which we speak, met with five propitious conjunctions under the constellation (Kathuttarái) Uttaraphálguni, which were as follows; he descended from above in Uttaraphálguni, and entered on the fœtal state; in Uttaraphálguni he was removed from one womb to another; he was born also; he was shaved likewise, and from being a householder became a houseless wanderer, and, lastly, in Uttaraphálguni*, he obtained that real

---

* The original of this Jain Gayatri is as follows :—

नमो अरीहंताणं नमो सिद्धाणं नमो आयरीयाणं
नमो उवज्झायाणं नमो लोए सव्व साहूणं

† In explanation of what is meant by being under a constellation, take the following example:—

Charitra Dvitiya, S. P., the second day of the Hindu year of Saka 1768, corresponding to March 29, 1846, was under the constellation Asvini, the first in the series; the next day, March 30, was under Bharani, the second of the series; and so on till all the twenty-seven constellations were completed, when the series began anew with the 28th day, or April 25. Each of these constellations are now divided into four parts, called feet,

and supreme wisdom and perception, which is infinite in its subjects, incomparable in its kind, imperturbable, free from all obscurity, a touchstone for all other things, and perfect in all its parts. It was under Sváti, however, that the lord obtained Nirván (cessation from action, and freedom from desire.)

In this age, and at that time, the adorable ascetic Mahávíra, in the summer season, in the fourth month, in the right demi-lunation, during the increasing moon of Ashádha, and on its sixth day, descended from the all-joyous super-celestial abode* called Pushpottara, which, like the lotus among flowers, is the chief of all the super-celestial abodes. There having remained twenty oceans of years, and expended the life destined for him in that place, having finished the actions of that state, and laid aside his celestial form, without the smallest interval of time, he descended to this earth in the continent of Jambudvípa, in the country of Bharata Varsha, that Bharata Varsha which lies to the south (of Meru), during the currency of this Avasarpini (age), after the Happy

---

viz., a golden, a silver, a brass, and an iron foot; each less lucky than the preceding.

* These are the abodes by the Jains called *Vimána,* a term used by the Brahmans for a celestial car, or any other kind of conveyance.

Happy age (consisting of four hundred billions of oceans of years) had passed, and the Happy age also (of three hundred billions), and the Happy mixed with Misery likewise (of two hundred billions), and the Miserable tinged with Happiness (of one hundred billions of oceans of years) was also spent, except forty-two thousand and seventy-four years, and eight months and a half, after twenty-one Tirthankars had been born, of the tribe of Ikshváku, and family of Kasyapa, and two in the Harivansa tribe, and family of Gautama. Twenty-three Tirthankars had then passed away, when the adorable ascetic Mahávíra*, the last of the Tirthankars, and pointed out as about to obtain this dignity by those who preceded him, took up his abode as a fœtus in the womb of the Bráhmani Devanandi, of the family of Jalandhara, wife of Rishabha Datta Bráhman, of the family of Kodala, of the city of Kundagám, at the middle of the night, at a fortunate conjunction of the moon and planets, having left his heavenly banquet, quitted his celestial abode, and laid aside his former body. In refer-

---

* The original of these epithets of Mahávíra so often used is समणे भगवन् They might perhaps be equally well rendered the Ascetic Lord. The Sanskrit translation is, तपस्वी ज्ञानवान्

ence to this transaction there are three kinds of knowledge the adorable ascetic Mahávíra may be supposed to have had; that he was to descend, *that* he had; that he was descending, *that* he had not; and that he had descended, *that* he had.

On that very night on which the adorable ascetic Mahávíra took the form of an embryo in the womb of Devanandi, of the family of Jalandhara, the same Devanandi was lying on her couch, and after sleeping a short time wakened up after seeing the following most excellent, prosperity-foreboding, evil-destroying, wealth-conferring, fortunate, delightsome objects in a dream. The objects were as follows: an elephant, a bull, a lion, the goddess Lakshmi, a garland of flowers, the moon, the sun, a military ensign, a large jar, the lotus lake, the sea (of milk), the celestial residence of the sages, a collection of pearls, a smokeless flame of fire*. Such were the fourteen most excellent, prosperity-foreboding, evil-destroying, wealth-conferring, fortunate, delightsome† dreams which Devanandi

---

* The original is as follows:—

गय वसह सीह अभिसेय दाम ससि दिणयरं झयं
कुभं पउमसरं सागर विमाणभवण रयणुच्चय सिहिच

† This and similar repetitions, with which the original abounds, I shall in future generally omit.

saw. Glad and delighted, and with a heart filled with joy, pleased and placid, while a sensation of pleasure stole through all her soul, like that which affects the kadamba blossoms when moistened by a shower of rain, with all the hairs of her body standing upright in their pores with delight, and keeping the dream firmly fixed in her mind, she got up from her couch. Then without hurry or precipitation, or perturbation of mind, and yet without delay, with the stately gait of a swan, she went to the place where Rishabha Datta Bráhman was, and saluting him by wishing him all joy*, sat down at her ease on a large comfortable seat, and then joining her hands, so as to bring the ten nails together, and having placed her joined hands on her forehead, she thus addressed him; "O beloved of the gods, to-night I was lying, slumbering on my couch, and after sleeping a very short time, I awoke after seeing fourteen remarkable dreams; they were an elephant, &c.; O beloved of the gods†, tell me what good fortune these visions portend." Thereon Rishabha Datta Bráhman, having care-

---

* जएणं विजयेणं वद्धावेद् is the original of this ancient form of salutation.

† This is the famous ancient title, Devánupiya, so common in Asoka's edicts, but which now by the Brahmans is applied to a silly or a crazy person, as if in contempt of the holders of the doctrine of Nirván.

fully apprehended the matter she had laid before him, glad and delighted; placing the dream fully before his mind, engaged in deep reflection, taxing all his powers till by an intellect that could look into all times, and a reason that comprehended all relations, he came to a full comprehension of the meaning of the dream, when he thus addressed Devanandi: "O beloved of the gods, you have seen a dream foreboding prosperity; beloved of the gods, a most fortunate dream; beloved of the gods, a pleasure-giving dream; a dream the source of felicity. This much is most certain, yes at the end of nine full months and seven and a-half nights*, a child shall be born with well-shaped hands and feet, perfect in every member of his body, with every lucky mark, mole, and characteristic†, pro-

---

* Like as in our fortnight and se'ennight, we have here time reckoned by nights.

† The commentator says that a Tirthankar has a hundred and eight marks, but other lucky persons have some or all of the following thirty-two on the palms of the hands or soles of of the feet:—A large umbrella, a lotus, a bow, chariot, club, tortoise, goad, well, the mark Svastica, a garland, tank, lion, tree, quoit, conch, an elephant, the sea, a temple, fish, grain of barley, plough, post, pitcher, king, leather-dresser, mirror, bull, flag, the goddess Lakshmi, a string of flowers, a peacock. Red nails, feet, hands, tongue, lips, palate, and eyes, he also tells us are unlucky. A man who has the forehead, breast, and mouth all large, will be a king. Such are some of the elements of the Jain palmistry and occult sciences.

portioned in height, weight, and thickness*, with every limb fully developed, and perfect in beauty, with a form resembling the moon, graceful and pleasing to the eye; to such an entirely lovely child will you give birth. On leaving the state of childhood†, he will be perfect in all the inferior branches of knowledge, and after entering on the state of youth, he will soon become able to repeat, defend, and uphold the four Vedas, the Rig Veda, Yajur Veda, Sáma Veda, and the Atharvana Veda, and the Itihása (Legendary History), which is considered a fifth Veda, and the Nighantu (Lexicon), which may be termed a sixth; the body of divinity with all its members, and know also their hidden meaning. He will be acquainted with the six subsidiary members of the Veda, and the sixth philosophical system (the Sánkhya), with the Mathematics, the Institute which directs in rites and ceremonies, Grammar, Prosody, Analysis of words, Astronomy, and other Brahmanical Scriptures, especially that relating to the state of an ascetic; in all of these he will become a proficient‡. Thou,

---

* So Mána, Unmána, and Pramána, are interpreted by the commentator.

† That is, till the age of eight.

‡ In this curious passage, giving an account of Brahmanical sacred literature in the fifth century of our era, it is remarkable that the agreement with the present state of that literature is perfect, with the striking discrepancy of omitting all notice of the

O beloved of gods, hast indeed seen a dream that forebodes prosperity." And so saying he again

Puráns. If the Itihása be the Puráns, as the commentator seems to think, and not the Mahabhárat, which, however, is frequently by the Brahmans, as here, called the fifth Veda, then there was but one Purána at the time, according to Professor Wilson's conjecture, from which all the rest, by subtractions and additions, have been manufactured. As the whole passage is an interesting one, I put down the original here, along with the Sanskrit translation:—

जुवणगमणुप्पते। रिउवेय। जउव्वेय। सामवेय। अथव्वणवेय। इतिहासपंचमाणं। निग्घंटुछट्ठाणं। संगोवंगगाणं। सरहस्साणं। चउक्कवेयाणं। सारए। वारए। धारए। सडंगवी। सट्ठितन्त विसारए। सिखाणे। सिखाकप्पे। वागरणे। छन्दे। निरुत्ते। जोइसामयणे। अणेसुय। बंभन्नएसु। परिवायएसु। सुपरिनिव्विट्ठिए। आवि भविस्सई॥

यौवनं अनुप्राप्तः। ऋग्वेद। यजुर्वेद। सामवेद। अथर्वणवेद। इतिहासपुराणं पंचमं येषां ते। निघंटु नामसंग्रहः षष्ठो येषां ते। संगो अंगोपांगसहितानां। तात्पर्ययुक्तानां ईदृशानां पूर्वोक्तानां चतुर्णां वेदानां स्मारकः। वारकः अंन्येषां अन्नपानान्निषेधी। धारणसमर्थः। पूर्वोक्तषडंगवित्। षष्टितन्त्रं कापिलशास्त्रं तत्रविशारदपंडितः। गणितशास्त्रकुशलः। यज्ञादिविधिशास्त्रे। विंशतिव्याकरणानि तेषु। छंदःशास्त्रे।

and again gave expression to his sympathetic joy. The Bráhmani Devanandi, on the other hand, having thus received the interpretation of her dream confidently believed it, and with a heart filled with gladness and delight, again joining her hands, and raising them to her forehead, thus addressed her husband: "So be it, O beloved of the gods, be it as thou hast said. No word of thine shall fail; all shall be established. My desire shall be accomplished. I embrace the words that have fallen from your lips. O beloved of the gods, I confide in the truth of the joyful announcement." Here then the matter rested, but while she was delightfully engaged in inquiring of Rishabha Datta into the meaning of these fortunate, pleasure-inspiring dreams, at the same time and season Sakra (Sakko), the chief and king of the gods, who holds in his hand the thunderbolt, is the destroyer of cities, the performer of a hundred sacrifices, has a thousand eyes, possesses all the materials for sacrifices, is the destroyer of the Daitya, lord of that half of the world that lies to the south (of Meru), who rides on Airávat, is prince of the Súras, and possessor of three hundred and twenty

---

पदव्युत्पत्तिरूपदेशकादौ। ज्योतिःशास्त्रे। अन्येषु च पूर्वोक्तेषु ब्राह्मणशास्त्रेषु परिव्राजकसंबंधिषु शास्त्रेषु अतिनिपुणा भविष्यति॥

thousand celestial abodes, is clothed in pure ethereial robes, whose head is encircled with a tiara, on whose cheeks fall down the circular ear-rings made of new gold, and delighting the beholder, possessed of great wealth, of great splendour, of great strength, of great fame, of great majesty, and enjoying great felicity, whose body shines with its own radiance, who has a garland of five kinds of flowers falling down on his breast, rightful sovereign of the heavenly mansions, rightful sovereign of other celestial abodes, rightful president of the divine council, who sits on the throne called (Sakra) "the mighty," who is lord of the gods who inhabit the three hundred and twenty thousand celestial mansions, of the eighty-four thousand equal gods, of the thirty-three superior, and those whom they receive into their company of the guardian divinities of the four worlds*, of the eight principal queens†, with their domestics, of the three councils, of the seven branches of the army‡ of the gods, who protect the lives of the eighty-four thousand divinities, and multitudes of gods and goddesses besides, to whom I say belongs the sovereignty, pri-

* The Lunar, the Infernal, and those of Varuña and Kuvera.

† Padmá, Sivá, Sachi, Anjá, Auralá, Navanriká, Rohini.

‡ Musicians, actors, horses, elephants, chariots, foot-soldiers, and baggage-bullocks, so says the Comment. This is different from the Brahmanical description of an army; but this, and many other curious points, must be left to the reflections of the reader acquainted with Brahmanical literature.

ority, chieftainship, presidency, and absolute command of all this vast army, directing and protecting all ; while then he was enjoying vocal music, the dance and the song, the sound of the pipe, the violin, the cymbal, the timbrel, the tambourine, and the loud-sounding drum, partaking of divine delight, he with a knowledge next to infinite* cast his eyes with an all-embracing view down on the continent of Jambudvípa, permitting them to roam all abroad till they lighted on the place where the adorable ascetic Mahávíra had just become incarnate, in the continent of Jambudvípa, in the region of Bharata Varsha, that part of Bharata which lies to the south (of Meru), in the city of Kundagráma, the Brahmanical division, in the womb of the Bráhmani Devanandi, of the tribe of Jalandhara, the wife of the Bráhman Rishabha Datta, of the tribe of Kodala. On beholding this, glad and delighted, and with a heart full of joy, elated and filled with pleasure, in a state of the most enchanting ecstacy, and with his whole soul absorbed in a transport of delight, and like the sweet-smelling kadamba blossoms after a shower of rain, having all the hairs of his body erect, like so many flowery filaments, blossoming in their pores, and with face and eyes resembling a full-blown lotus, the beautiful bracelets and carved armlets, which he wore shak-

---

* In the original, *like* infinite. It is only Tirthankars who have infinite knowledge.

ing on him, his tiara, his long ear-rings, and the garland which adorned his breast, and all the jewels with which he was ornamented thrown into commotion, he descends in haste from his throne, steps down from the footstool, and advancing several paces, Indra, lord of the celestials, clad in his robes of honour, and adorned with all his jewels, loosed from his feet the shoes ornamented with dark shining lapis-lazuli stones, and other jewels, set in them by a divine artist, and throwing his seamless robe* over his left shoulder, and joining his hands so as to bring the nails together, he advanced still seven or eight steps in the direction of the Tirthankar, when kneeling so as to keep his left knee up, while his right was on the ground, he bowed his head three times to the earth, keeping it each time for a short period in the posture of adoration, and afterwards raising his arms with the hands so united as to bring the nails together, and thus carrying them up to his forehead, he spoke as follows: "Adoration to the venerable†, worshipful‡ performer of all previous works§, who

---

* एगसालोअं *i. e.* अखण्डवस्त्र:

† Arihant.

‡ Bhagaván.

§ Aígara *Sans.* Adhikára, a name given to Brahma Deva by Brahmans, but here to be understood as above; the reason given by the commentator for performance of works being स्वतीर्थापेक्षा

procures the means of salvation*, the self-instructed†, the best of men, the lion among men‡, the chief lotus among men§, the leading elephant among men, the best of mortals, the leader of mortals, like a lamp hung up among mortals, the irradiator of mortals, the bestower of perfect security, who bestows intellectual vision, the establisher of the way of life, the giver of easy access, the giver of life, the great teacher, the establisher of religion, the giver of religious instruction, the lord of religion, the charioteer of religion, the emperor of those who have entered on the four religious states, the saviour of a continent, the asylum of those who apply to him, the receiver of those who seek indestructible wisdom, who is free from all fraud and violence, the conqueror of himself, and teaching others to conquer themselves, the saviour of himself, and the saviour of others, himself perfect in wisdom, and imparting wisdom to others, the emancipator of himself, and the emancipator of others, possessed of omniscience, seeing all existent beings, free from pain and instability, from disease and decay, and not liable to injuries, possessed of

---

* Tirthankara, which I explain as above.

† Sayamsambuddhánam परोपदेशं विना

‡ To tear mercilessly the passions.

§ To cover them with his protection, as the lotus does the water with its leaves.

infinitude, and who does not return again to the world, who is named the obtainer of perfection, and has reached the highest place of dignity. Adoration to the victor, who has in his breast the assurance of victory, I adore the worshipful, venerable Mahávíra, who has performed all the preliminary virtuous acts, and is the last of the Tirthankars, pointed out by all the former Tirthankars, and who has at last obtained the supreme object of desire. I prostrate myself before the all-venerable, who now seems to me gone thither, and present here ; O Lord, both here and there, I adore thee." So saying, he returned and took his seat on his throne. After a little while, reflecting within himself on the subject before him, the following thoughts occurred to the mind of Sakra*, prince and king of the gods; Surely such a thing as this has never happened in past, happens not in present, nor will happen in future time, that an Arhat, a Chakravarti, a Baladeva, or a Vasudeva should be born in a low caste family, a servile family, a degraded family, a poor family, a mean family, a beggar's family, or a Brahman's family; but, on the contrary, in all time past, present, and

* In Mágadhi *Sakko*, the common name of Indra among writers in this and the Pali language. The word is much the same as "The Almighty," used as a name for the Deity, which in Indra corresponds to "Lord."

to come, an Arhat*, a Chakravarti†, a Vasudeva‡, receives birth in a noble family, an honorable family, a royal family, a Kshatriya family, as in the family of Ikshváku, or the Harivansha family, or some such of pure descent. Now truly there threatens to take place a wonder which has never happened, nor does happen, nor will happen in the world throughout the course of infinite Utsarpinis§, and Avasarpinis. His first origin, the act of giving him a family name, must be such as to consort with an undecaying, indescribable, indestructible renown. I say, then, that the birth of an Arhat, a Chakravarti, a Baladeva, or a Vasudeva has not taken place, nor does, nor will take place in a low caste, servile, contemptible, poor, beggarly, miserly, or Brahman family, such a thing neither was, is, nor shall be, and yet the venerable ascetic Mahávíra has just now descended to the continent of Jambudvípa, the country of Bharata, to the Brahman division of the town of Kundagráma, and

---

* The highest class of sages among the Jains, are worthy of divine honours.

† In *Mágadhi*, Chakkavatti, an emperor, a king who has other kings under him.

‡ The Jains make Krishna and others belong to the class of demigods styled Vasudevas; Bala Ráma they make a Baladeva, a still inferior kind of demigod.

§ Immense cycle of ages. See Preface.

is conceived in the womb of Devanandi, the wife of Rishabha Datta; wherefore he is now about doing a thing that never happened, nor does, nor will happen, during the presidency of any Indra, prince and king of the gods, that an Arhat should be born in a low caste, or Brahman family, and not on the contrary in a noble family. The best thing then that can be done is to withdraw the venerable ascetic Mahávíra, last of the Tirthankars, and pointed out by his predecessors, from the womb of Devanandi, and place him in that of Tris'alá, the Kshatrayin, of the family of Vasishta, wife of Siddhártha, the Kshatriya, of the family of Kasyapa, both of pure Kshatriya descent*. After these thoughts had passed through his mind, he called Harinegamesi, the chief of his messengers, and thus addressed him: "O beloved of the gods, a thing now threatens to take place, which never happened before, nor now happens, nor ever will happen, that the birth of an Arhat should

---

* It is difficult to say what could have induced the author to invent this ridiculous story, (unless it were to vent his spite against the Brahmans), so like the Puranic legend of Balarama's transference. In this fable Harinegamesi acts the part that the Brahmans assign to Yoganidrá. The commentator anticipates objections to the story, and brings forward the Brahmanical legend to support the credit of the author. The two stories are no doubt connected, but it may be doubted which is the original.

take place in a low caste, or Brahmanical family. Therefore go you, O beloved of the gods, to the worshipful ascetic Mahávíra, who is now conceived in the womb of Devanandi, in the Brahman division of the city of Kundagráma, and withdraw him from thence, and place him in the womb of Trisalá, the wife of Siddhártha, and return quickly, and report your diligence in this affair." Harinegamesi*, chief of the heavenly messengers, having received the commands of Sakra, king and chief of the gods, delighted, and with a heart filled with joy, bringing his hands together (in token of obedience), immediately addressed himself to the execution of the orders which he had received from the mouth of the god. Having accordingly gone to the north-east quarter, he, at the commencement of his journey, changed his appearance, exhibiting himself in the form of a pillar of innumerable leagues in length, combining the lustre of the diamond, the ruby, the emerald, the opal, the pulaka†, Sugandha, Jyotivanta, Anjana, Anjanapula, Jyotiresa, Subhaga, Anka, rock crystal, amethyst, and other brilliant gems, and of the consistency of muslin. After thus proceeding a certain space, he

* The Sanskrit given here is Harinaigamaishi. I suppose the name means "swifter than a deer."

† I give here the Sanskrit names of those gems of which I cannot ascertain any thing certain.

again changed his appearance, and assuming an atomic body, he darted with a motion graceful, rapid, willing, exultant, fleet, elegant, in a word, entirely perfect and divine, through seas and continents till he arrived at Jambudrípa, at the house of Rishabha Datta. On entering, he at once saw the worshipful ascetic Mahávíra, and prostrated himself before him. Then having cast Devanandi, with all her attendants and family, into a deep sleep*, having removed all impure matter, he took out what was pure, and without injuring or paining the adorable ascetic Mahávíra, he placed him surrounded with a divine lustre, in the palm of one hand, and covering him with the other, carried him off to the Kshatriya division of Kundagráma, to the house of the Kshatriya Siddhártha, where was his wife Trisalá; having then cast her and her attendants into a deep sleep, without injury or pain, he introduced the adorable ascetic Mahávíra in the womb of the Kshatrayín. When he had performed this service, he returned with a graceful, divine motion through seas and continents, thousands of leagues, till he reached the abodes of the blessed, and entered the heaven of the religious†, where

* This by the Jains is called Asvápani Nidrá, and it is the deepest of the three kinds of sleep which they reckon up, putting one in mind of a mesmeric sleep.

† Called "Sandharmávantaraloka Viman."

is the throne of Sakra, the chief and king of the gods, and reported to his lord that he had performed what he was commanded to do. In reference to this transaction, the adorable ascetic may be supposed to have had three kinds of knowledge, but in reality he knew that he was to be withdrawn, and that he was withdrawn, but he did not know when he was in the act of being withdrawn.

CHAPTER II.

TRISALÁ'S DREAMS.

IN the same night that the adorable ascetic Mahávíra was removed to the womb of Trisalá, she was lying in her splendid mansion, ornamented inside with numerous paintings, and outside with smooth white stucco, having a ceiling adorned underneath with various colours, and with clusters of darkness-dispelling pearls, and a floor perfectly smooth, and marked with lucky figures, in which were bouquets of fresh and sweet-smelling flowers of all the five different colours, along with black aloe wood, and the finest frankincense and ambergris, burning and sending up curling scented fumes, inspiring delight, and making the house emit an odour like a grove of frankincense trees; in such a splendid mansion, on a couch large enough to allow the body to be stretched at full length, with pillows at head and foot, and raised at the sides, while flat in the middle, with a foot-stool to mount it, soft as the sand on the banks of the Ganges, with sheets of the finest materials, thrown over it*, with a handkerchief lying on it of the richest colours, covered with mosquito curtains, in a word, altogether delightsome, soft to the touch as fur, silk, cotton, or butter, and scented with sandal-wood, and other sweet-smelling woods, altogether a couch to be coveted, there, while lying, and having fallen asleep but a short time, about the middle of the night, she saw the same fourteen propitious dreams that the Brahmani Devanandi saw, after which she wakened up. The objects seen by her in her dreams were, first, an elephant with four tusks, looking like radiant drops of dew, or a heap of pearls, or the sea of milk, possessing a radiance like the moon, huge as the silvery mountain Vaitádhya†, while from his temples oozed out the sweet liquid that attracts the swarms of bees. Such was the incomparably stately elephant, equal to Airávat himself, which Queen Trisalá saw, while uttering a fine deep sound, with his trunk filled with water, like the sound of thunder; in every respect an incomparable elephant.

She next saw a bull shedding a flood of radiance, like to that which proceeds from a bunch

---

* *Sans.* चौमं अतिसीयं which should be linen or silk; but the Gujarathi makes the covering of cotton stuff.

† A fabulous mountain, which the Jains suppose first to receive and then reflect the sun's rays.

of white lotus flowers, shining and darting out rays on every side. A very fine ornamental attractive hump adorned his shoulders. His skin was clear, his hair sleek, his form graceful, and his body in good condition, and altogether beautiful to look on ; his horns were circular, smooth, and elevated; his teeth were harmless and clean. Such was the assemblage of excellent qualities the bull possessed.

She next saw a lion of a dazzling white colour, like a bunch of pearls, or the sea of milk, or the lunar radiance, or the drops of dew, whiter than the great mountain Vaitádhya, pleasing and delightful to the sight, strong, muscular, and fat, with his members all properly rounded in the most elegant way, having a sharp well-formed jaw, a mouth beautiful as the periphery of a lotus, a fine muscular lip, with a palate like the red water lily, and the tip of his tongue hanging out of his mouth like fine gold being poured out of a crucible, while his bright eye seemed like a ball of lightning falling upon you. His chest was broad, and his large well-made shoulders were adorned with a soft, bright, fine, sleek, long-haired mane, while his tail was raised aloft with a circle in the centre*, bounding like a ball, and possessing the good qualities as well as form of the moon. He seemed bounding play-

* This is the form intended 

fully along, and descending from heaven with open mouth, as if he were coming directly down upon you; a lion with sharp strong claws, yet pleasing to the sight, and with a tongue hanging out of his mouth, beautiful as the petal of a lotus.

The fourth dream seen by her whose face was like the full moon, was a vision of the goddess Lakshmí, sitting on her lofty lotus throne. Her form was altogether excellent; one foot was firmly planted on the ground, and seemed like a pillar of gold. It was elevated in the centre like the back of a tortoise, while the nails partly hid by the muscles of the toes, were stained with a brilliant red dye. Her fingers and toes were soft and tapering like the leaves of a lotus; her well-formed legs were adorned with circular ornaments; her knee-bones were hid in the muscles, and her thighs tapering upward like the trunk of an elephant. Encircling her loins was an elegant zone of gold, while the circle of the navel resembled a cloud of black bees, being continuous, fine, ever-moving, soft, downy, large, and elegant. The other three circles which are in the middle of the palms of the hands, were also elegantly formed. Her whole body was adorned with various kinds of jewels, wholly faultless, and highly brilliant. In particular, she had a pearl necklace, intermingling with garlands of sweet-scented flowers. A circular pendant fell down between her breasts, and adorned her chest, on which it rested. She had also around her neck a string of grains and golden dinars*. Two large ear-rings hung down from her ears, and illumined the shoulders with which they came in contact. Every thing about her was beautiful; her face had a noble aspect; her eyes were large and lovely, like lotus flowers; she held a water lily, still dripping with water, in her hand, and she was fanned by an agreeable wind, which set in motion her fine black braided hair. Such was the goddess the queen saw residing in her lotus house, called *Padmadraha,* on the top of Mount Himávat, and by whom stood the guardian elephant of that quarter of the heavens, bathing her with water from his trunk.

The fifth dream was a vision of a garland of flowers altogether delightsome, and worthy a place in the heaven of delights. It was composed of the following flowers—champaka, asoka, punnága, priyangu, sarisava, magara†, málati†, játi†, juhi†, kolla, koshta, and bakula, intermingled with amaranth

---

* The original word is here retained दीनार The custom of stringing coins together, and adorning with them children especially, is still very common in India.

† These are all varieties of Jasmine. The scientific names of the other flowers will generally be found in WILSON's *Dictionary*.

leaves, and southern-wood, besides jasmine of other rare varieties; and sesame flowers, and other flowers of spring, with red, blue, and white water lilies, with beautiful sweet-smelling mango blossoms—producing altogether an unequalled, delightsome, sweet-smelling garland of flowers, imparting pleasure to the inhabitants of the ten regions of the world, shining and waving, and pleasing the eye, and of every variety of colour, while a swarm of six-footed* honey-bees were seen buzzing and flying around it as it descended from heaven.

The queen next saw the moon white as the froth of milk, the drops of dew†, or a silver spire, rejoicing the heart, delighting the eyes, a perfect circle, destroying thick conglomerated, impenetrable darkness, a full moon, at the exact point between the two halves of the month, bringing out the radiance of the wild lotus flowers, adorning night, shining like a polished mirror, and brilliant as the white swan, sharpening the arrows

---

* The Jains are fond of four-tusked elephants and six-footed bees, and other such preter-natural animals.

† दगरय literally *water-pearls*, both Sanskrit and Gujarathi give जलकणाः The Sanskrit from which the Magádhi is changed may be उदकरज as well as उदकरत्न

of Cupid, and raising the oceanic tides*, not to be looked on by disconsolate wives temporarily separated from their husbands, lest they suffer a greater calamity; a moon altogether lovely, like the mark on the forehead, the pride of all the circling starry host, especially beloved of Rohini in soul and heart. Such was the glorious lovely full moon which Trisalá saw.

She next in her dream saw the sun, rending the curtain of night, all glorious with his encircling radiance, like a bunch of red asoka or palása flowers, like the bill of a parrot, or the red side of the retti seed, adorning the beds of wild lotuses, occupying his proper station in the beginning of the ecliptic, like a lamp hung down from heaven, destroying the influence of cold; the prince of planets, the conqueror of night, who at his rising and setting comes near us, but afterwards removes far from us, who disperses the evil doers that stroll about in the dark, who stops the influence of the cold winds, who circles round Meru the

---

* The original here is समुद्दरगपूरगं The Sanskrit translation is समुद्रजलवेलावर्द्धकं I mention this in case of any doubting whether the author knew the true cause of the rise of the tides, especially as I do not recollect seeing it mentioned any where, that the ancient Hindus understood this subject.

prince of mountains, the mighty Súrya, darting forth his thousand rays, the glory of the Aditya.

Next she saw a standard, with its golden staff firmly fixed, and its flag, consisting of a profusion of blue, red, yellow, and white cloth, raised and spread out to the wind, while the extremity was adorned with a bunch of peacock's feathers. It was brilliant as crystal, a pure conch, the flowers of jasmine, the drops of dew, or a silver jar. Its head was in the shape of a lion's, exceedingly splendid, while it pierced the sky with its extremity. It was lucky to behold, and had its soft flag moved backward and forward by a gentle wind, and, though vast in size, yet of a form attractive to the beholder.

She next saw a jar shining like burnished gold, full of the purest and best water, brilliant and ornamental, and placed upon a lotus made of pearls, delighting the eyes, and shedding a brilliant lustre, which diffused itself on all sides; a habitation of the mild Lakshmí herself, wholly free of defect, fortunate, and resplendent, a very type of prosperity, having the beautiful and sweet-smelling flowers of all seasons arranged in it like a necklace: altogether, a perfect and brilliant flower-pot.

She next saw the Lotus Lake, irradiated by the first beams of the rising sun, which tinged its waters with an orange hue, producing innumerable thousand-leaved water lilies, filled with aquatic animals, and exhibiting shoals of happy fishes, sporting and shining as if the water were on fire. There sprung up lotuses of the solar radiance and of the lunar radiance, the blue lotus, the rose-coloured, and the pale, all growing together in one inartificial, splendid, delighful assemblage. Large black bees, and swarms of gadflies, were luxuriating among the leaves. Black swans, and white swans, cranes, geese, and Indian cranes, in all their pride, males and females, were fluttering over the water, while the lotus leaves, besprinkled with drops of dew, reflected every variety of colour, a sight wholly pleasing to the eye; a piece of water inspiring the highest delight.

She next saw the sea of milk shining like the moon, when she shines with her utmost brilliance, propitious as the divine curl*, the fluid rushing together from the four quarters of the heavens, the lofty waves incapable of measurement†, utterly devoid of stability, agitated by the tempestuous winds; in one place rushing against each other, while in another they dash against the shore, sending forth a brilliant spray, inspiring the

---

* Srívatsa, considered lucky among Jains and Brahmans.

† So I paraphrase आत्मप्रमाणा: a fine idea, "that can be compared only to themselves."

soul with delight. Enormous whales, crocodiles, and sea-serpents*, darting through the fluid, form rivers of foam, white as camphor; and again diving into the depths, occasion a whirlpool, like that of the Ganges when she bursts through her mountain barriers. Such was the mighty effervescence of waters seen by the queen, whose countenance was radiant as the moon.

After this she saw a celestial mansion†, resplendent and shining with a radiance like that of the newly risen sun, or a large heap of pearls, with a hundred and eight pillars, each shedding a flood of light from the gold and jewels with which they were adorned. It seemed a lamp let down from heaven, or some radiant celestial garland. Upon it were painted lions‡, oxen, horses, men, alligators, fishes, serpents, heavenly choristers, celestial roebucks, and eight-legged deer§, Tibetan cows, elephants, and many other animals. It was ornamented also with the finest flowers, and great

---

* Timingala, Nirudha, Tilira.

† The original is Vimána, but the Jains use this word for a mansion, and not for a car.

‡ मग for मृगाः the commentator has strangely वृकाः the Guj. is सीयाल

§ रुरु the Jains consider these to have eight-legs.

variety of lotuses. The heavenly band of singers sent forth a sound, articulate and harmonious, yet so loud that the thunder which issues from some immense lightning-charged watery cloud could not equal it; while the celestial bass drum sends forth a sound not inferior to that which all the men and animals in the world could raise. The finest aloe-wood, and incense, and ignited ambergris, send up a fragrant smoke, which, rising in curling wreaths, delights by its sweet perfumes, ever continuing radiant and bright, and diffusing abroad streams of delight; a mansion in every respect desirable for the gods. Such was the splendid lotus habitation seen by the queen.

The next thing seen was a heap of jewels. It contained diamonds, adamants*, sapphires, chalcedonies, rubies, emeralds, corals, rock crystals, fragrant stones, swan-egg stones, black jewels, moon stones, and other precious stones, piled together in an immense heap, and illuminating heaven with their radiance, a heap of jewels high even as Meru, prince of mountains.

Last of all she saw the smokeless fire, large, bright, and of an orange colour, fed by fresh

* These are respectively पुलग and वेरिदं. Some of the following are mere translations of names without imparting any knowledge of what stones they refer to, a thing I am unable to do.

E 2

melted butter, blazing away without producing any smoke. The flame was most pleasant to the sight, rising and falling alternately, a mass of fire coming out of itself and again returning into itself; a swift ever-flitting fire, with a flame rising aloft, extending itself on all sides, seeming as if it were about to bake the firmament*.

---

* अंवरं कच्चद्रूपयंतं that is आकाशपचनसमर्थं.

CHAPTER III.

THE COURT OF SIDDHÁRTHA.

SUCH were the prosperity-foreboding dreams which when the lotus-eyed queen, mother of the Tirthankar, had seen, she wakened up; and, fixing the dreams firmly in her memory, and descending from her couch by means of the footstool, went to the place where the Kshastriya Siddhártha was lying in his bed asleep. There serenading him with her gentle and sweet voice, in these words:—"Thou art most noble, most amiable, most beloved, most worthy of being thought on and delighted in, most mighty, prosperous, gentle, wealthy, bounteous, fortunate, and worthy of all the affection of the heart, the disperser of hostile armies*,"—she

* In the original these are all epithets of गिराहिं that is, गीर्भिः but I am informed that the meaning is as given, and such an enumeration of the qualities of a great man by an officer who goes before, is still a necessary part of Hindu ceremonial on public occasions.

awaked him out of his sleep. Thereon King Siddhártha graciously receiving her, commanded her to sit down on an elegant easy seat, adorned with gold and jewels; whence she, after being seated, thus in sweet accents addressed him:—"O my lord, while I was this evening sleeping in my splendidly furnished apartments, I saw the following objects in a dream, viz., an elephant, a bull, &c. Tell me then, my lord, what good fortune and future happiness these fourteen dreams forebode." King Siddhártha, glad and delighted, after fully grasping with his mind, and reflecting again and again on the dreams, while he summoned up all his powers of intellect and reason, having comprehended their meaning, thus explained it to Trisalá:—"O beloved of the gods, thou hast seen a prospering, propitious, blessed dream, a dream that portends good fortune, and happiness that forebodes the birth of a royal son. In nine months and seven and a half days, thou wilt give birth to a heaven-descended son, who will become an ensign to our family, the lamp of our family, the family crown, the family frontal ornament*, the enricher of the family, the stay of the family, the sun of the family, the glory of the

* Tilaka, a lucky ornamental round mark Hindus make with a paste on their forehead.

family, the family foundation, and the family exalter. His hands and feet will be perfect in beauty, his five senses perfect, and all his qualities, properties, and marks*, complete, of proper height, weight, and proportions, and all the limbs properly developed, and agreeable to the sight as the moon. Such shall be thy son; and when he passes from the state of childhood to that of youth, he will be perfect in all the common branches of knowledge, and as a youth will be brave, heroic, powerful, well built, capable of leading armies; in a word, a king of kings. Thou hast seen, therefore, a most propitious dream;"—and this he repeated two or three times.

When then Trisalá had heard the interpretation of the dream from King Siddhártha, laying it up in her heart, and bringing her joined hands to her forehead, she thus spoke:—"I accept of the interpretation you have given as wholly free from error and doubt, and as altogether excellent and according to my wishes." So saying, she rose from her seat, and departed; but, on reflection, she said in her own mind, "Now, I must take care that no wicked dream follow, to destroy the virtue of this one. Dreams concerning the gods,

---

* That is, moles and marks on the body, which are considered of great importance.

religious teachers, and things good, lucky, charitable and desirable, require that a person should afterwards continue watching." She thus accordingly acted.

In the morning, at the first dawning of the day, Siddhártha called some of the royal messengers*, and spoke to them as follows:—"O beloved of the gods, go now quickly without the palace, and prepare the hall of audience†, for holding a court to-day. Let the place be sprinked with scented water, and the floor newly smeared‡, let the hall be adorned with sweet-smelling flowers of the five different colours, let the best aloe-wood and ambergris and incense, send up in curling wreaths their sweet delight-inspiring perfumes. After the whole has been properly perfumed, let my throne be set down in the midst of it; and when you, by yourselves and others, have performed all these my commands, come back quickly and so report to

---

* *Mag.* कोडंबिअपुरिसे *Sans.* कौडंबिकपुरुषान् *Guj.* आदेशकारी

† उवठाणसालं a temporary building, or one of slight materials, large and spacious, such as the Hindus now construct, or deck out, on great occasions, a pavilion.

‡ That is, with cow-dung, as the Hindus do constantly to earthen floors, which, when dried and swept, are far from offensive, even to a European.

me." The messengers having thus received the commands of King Siddhártha, and laid up his words in their joyful hearts, joining their hands, said, "We have with all humility heard your commands, O our Lord, and will yield implicit obedience." Immediately they departed, and going to the hall of audience without the palace, prepared it as the king had ordered, and returning, so reported to his Majesty. Siddhártha arose, and by the help of his footstool descended from his couch, while it was yet the season of blooming early morn, and the brilliant aurora-like beds of full-blown flowers and lotuses appear in all their beauty, diffusing a radiance resembling red asoka flowers, rottleria blossoms, or the red phœnisia; and soon the rising sun, like the crimson side of the retti seed, the eyes and feet of the wild pigeon, or the scarlet-coloured eye-balls of the India cuckoo, emulating a bouquet of red China roses, deep as the colour of red lead, or that of a bunch of red lotuses, with his thousand rays, introducing day, and dispelling night and all its gloom, shines forth, and, like the red mark that adorns the forehead of children and women, irradiates the world of living creatures. Having got up, he went into the gymnasium*, where there was a profusion of instru-

---

* *M.* अट्टणशाला

ments for exercising the body, and weights for stretching the arms. There, after exercising himself till he was tired and tired again, he took various kinds of oil, some with a hundred and others with a thousand drugs and medicaments dissolved in them, sweet-smelling, nourishing, irradiating, exhilarating, fattening, strengthening, and quickening all the senses; he anointed himself all over with these; he was then well rubbed and shampoed by men skilled in the art, and who could impart a softness and tenderness even to the palms of the hands and soles of the feet, who could perform their work with quickness and dexterity, the first and cleverest of their profession, and who had studied well the art, and were incapable of fatigue, kneading the body till the bones were invigorated, the muscles refreshed, the skin relaxed, and the hair made to shine, all the four tissues of the body refreshed, and all languor and fatigue banished. He then left the gymnasium, and went into the bathing room*. The room was hung round with strings of pearls, and various kinds of jewels, the floor of the smoothest stucco-work; a delightful bathing place it was. Siddhártha sat down upon the jewelled easy bathing seat, and then performed his ablutions, so con-

* मज्जनघर

ducive to health and comfort, with tepid water, scented with flowers and sweet perfumes, pure water from a holy place. At the end of this operation, attended with so much pleasure, he dried himself with a towel made of soft, valuable, and finely coloured cloth. After this, he put on his robes, made of the most expensive materials, and fringed with jewels, entirely new, and adorned with wreaths of flowers, sprinkled with saffron, and scented with sandal-wood. He then threw around his neck, so as to fall down on his breast, a necklace, in which pearls and jewels and gold medals were intermingled with one another, consisting of eighteen, nine, or three strings, as the case might be. He next fitted his jewelled collar close to his neck*, put the rings on his fingers, and the armlets and bracelets on his muscular arms, while the long circular ear-rings hung down and adorned his cheeks, and a tiara his head. Thus arrayed, with the necklace adorning his breast, jewelled rings of the best gold his fingers, with an elegant scarf falling down on the left side, and with what is called the hero's ornament on his arm, made of the finest gold, and set with the most ex-

* These are two completely different pieces of dress; the former hangs loose like a garland, the latter fits close like a collar.

pensive jewels by the most skilful workmen, shining, glittering incomparable, in a word, like the tree that yields all that is desired, covered with ornaments, with a state umbrella held over his head, resembling a canopy of amaranth blossoms, and fanned with a chowrie, while the people raised an auspicious shout of triumph, attended by the commanders of the troops, and heads of departments, the vice-regent*, the heads of the police†, chief of the royal messengers†, counsellors, inferior and superior, astrologers, warders, cabinet ministers, slaves, and personal attendants, citizens, with the lawyers and bankers, commanders of the forces, commanders of the chariots, couriers, and sealers§, issued forth the king and lord of men,

---

* This is the Yuva raja, called in the text simply राइसर

† In India usually called the Kotwal; perhaps under the native governments, a commander of the city-guard would give a truer notion of his dignity.

‡ The Kodambia again; the Sanscrit is कुटम्बस्वामिनः the word कुटम्ब is not in the Dictionary, and it occurs too frequently to be erroneously written. Their dignity seems to have been much higher than that of the दूत mentioned afterwards.

§ संधिवाल whose duty it was, according to the king's command, to affix the royal signet to public documents. Such an officer, I believe, exists at the East India House.

the bull and lion among men, lovely to behold* as the moon after emerging from a large white cloud, shining among the surrounding stars and planets, and came outside to the place where the hall of audience was, and sat down upon his throne, which was placed so as to face the east. In the north-east quarter were placed eight seats of honour, covered with cloth, white as the flowers of the white mustard plant. Beyond these again, at a respectful distance, there was drawn a curtain fringed with jewels, and of the finest city manufacture, embroidered with images of stags, bulls, horses, men, crocodiles, birds, serpents, heavenly choristers, eight-legged deer, Tibetan cows, and elephants, with forest flowers and water lilies, forming a perfect screen from the multitude. Within this was set a throne, covered with the purest white cloth, and fringed with gold and jewels, for Queen Trisalá, soft and easy to sit on. Having then called the royal messengers, King Siddhártha thus addressed them:—"O beloved of the gods, go quickly and call a sage skilled in the Institute of the eight kinds of prognostics†, learned

---

* This is the famous epithet पियदसणे that occurs so frequently in the ancient inscriptions, and which we have here met with several times before.

† According to the Annotator, the eight kinds of prognostics are, those derived from the body, dreams, sounds, the earth,

in all the Sástras, and especially skilled in the interpretation of dreams." Having received the royal commands with reverence, the messengers, pleased and delighted, and having raised their hands to their foreheads in token of obedience, took their departure, and went into the middle of the city of Kundagráma, where lived the skilful interpreters of dreams.

---

moles and marks, congenital qualities and marks, meteoric portents, and heavenly portents. An example given is, that the twitching of the right eye, or the throbbing in the right side, is lucky to a man, and in the left to a woman, and the contrary. In the play of the Toy Cart it is singular that Arya's right arm throbbed when he escaped from danger, and Vasantsená's right eye twinkled when she fell into danger. Twitching in the throat he tells us portends finding a wife, in the legs fetters, in the head a kingdom, &c. The falling of a star betokens distress to subjects, and the occurrence of a hurricane causes disasters to kings. Laughing in a dream portends grief, and dancing bonds; with the exception of a cow, horse, elephant, or image everything black seen in a dream is unlucky, and everything white lucky, except cotton and wool. Such are some specimens of this precious Sástra.

CHAPTER IV.

THE INTERPRETERS OF DREAMS AT COURT.

ON entering the houses of the interpreters of dreams, the royal messengers delivered to them the King's message. On being thus summoned by the messengers of the noble Siddhártha, glad and delighted in heart, they first bathed, and performed the worship of the gods*, then, to prevent any prodigy or misfortune, put the lucky mark on their foreheads (Tilaka), put on clean, fortunate, courtly garments, good, light, and valuable; adorned their persons with jewels, and put on their heads the sesame seed and kusa grass, the insurers of good fortune. Thereon they left their houses, and went to the place, in the middle of Kundagráma, where King Siddhártha's palace was; there they stopped at the principal gate, distinguished by a crest in the shape of a crown, and having waited till all were collected, they

---

* This is omitted in one copy; but these men were probably by religion Bráhmans.

went together to the splendid hall of audience, where King Siddhártha was, and made obeisance to him, wishing him a continuance of prosperity and victory*. The King returned their salutations with all manner of respect, and ordered them to be seated on the aforementioned eight seats. Having also made Trisalá sit down with her maids of honour in the place prepared for her, with a sweet-smelling flower in his hand, in pleasing and gentle accents, he thus addressed the interpreters of dreams:—"O beloved of the gods, the noble Trisalá, to-night, after having slept a short time, saw, in her own splendid apartments, the following fourteen dreams: An elephant, a bull [*as before*]. Tell me what particular good fortune, and special felicity, these dreams portend." Thereupon the interpreters of dreams, with glad and joyous hearts, having heard the request of the noble Siddhártha, took the subject into consideration, reflected upon it, conversed on it with one another, and asked one another questions, till they had made out satisfactorily its hidden meaning; when, in the presence of King Siddhártha, one of them,

---

* जएणविजयेणवद्धावेति Instead of this simple form of blessing, the Commentator gives the following: "May you be happy, safe, rich, long-lived, have a numerous offspring, and always victorious, and may the Jain religion be always in your family." Also he gives another, which concludes thus: "May you live for ever,—live as long as the world lasts."

citing the texts from the Institute of Dreams, spoke as follows:—"O beloved of the gods, we have diligently searched the Institute of Dreams, and find that there are forty-two common dreams, and thirty extraordinary dreams, in all seventy-two. And it is further said, that the mother of an Arhat (highest order of Jain saint), or Chakravarti (emperor), sees fourteen of the thirty extraordinary dreams at the period of such child's conception. It is further stated that the mother of a Vasudeva, on such an occasion, sees seven, and then awakes; and the mother of a Baladeva, four; while the mother of a Mandalika Raja (dependent king), sees one. Since, then, O beloved of the gods, the noble Trisalá has seen the whole of the fourteen propitious dreams; this portends the obtaining of wealth, the obtaining of felicity, the obtaining of a son, the obtaining of joy, the obtaining of sovereignty,—and all this, O beloved of the gods, without any sort of doubt. Accordingly, after nine months and seven and a half days, the noble Trisalá will bring forth a son, who shall be a royal standard to his family, ... [*as in the last chapter*], an emperor of the four regions of the world, a conqueror of the passions, and also emperor of the four virtues*. Such, O

* These virtues are Dána, Síla, Tapa, and Bhava; or almsgiving, the exercise of compassion, the practice of fasting and

beloved of the gods, is the purport of the propitious dreams the noble Trisalá saw."

When King Siddhártha had heard these things from the interpreters of dreams, laying them up in his joyful and delighted heart, and bringing together and raising his hands to them in token of respect, he thus spoke:—"O beloved of the gods, be it even so as you have said—let all you have predicted happen without fail. The interpretation you have given is just such as one could desire, equal to their highest aspirations, and, I have no doubt, in accordance with perfect veracity." Having then loaded them with sweetmeats, sweet-smelling garlands, garments, ornaments, and such gifts as were due to them, King Siddhártha, with the highest reverence and honour, dismissed the interpreters of dreams*.

---

other austerities, the entire subjugation of the mind. In the works of the Buddhists the chief virtues are reckoned three, the third of these being omitted. This is a different thing, however, from the three principles of Buddhism.

* The Annotator here takes occasion to introduce a story, so good in itself, and so like one told of a debate that happened in the presence of King James, between a *canny Scot* and a Spanish doctor, that I here give a literal translation of it. There lived in the city of Paithan a learned man, who after expending thirty years in the study of the sciences became so puffed up with pride, that he stuck into his head-dress an elephant's hook as a flag of defiance, bound a belt round his stomach lest he

After he had done this, he went to the place within the curtain, where Queen Trisalá sat, and

---

should burst from the knowledge he contained, had a servant carrying a ladder, to bring down from heaven the vanquished disputant, who might there try to conceal his defeat, had with him also a pickaxe, to dig out the disputant who should skulk away to *Hades*, and a bundle of grass for the man to eat after his discomfiture, who should venture to throw at him the garland of defiance. Thus accoutred he travelled through the Deccan, Gujarath, and Marwar, vanquishing all who entered the lists with him. He went eveu as far as the banks of the Sarasvati, where hearing of the fame of Bhoja's Court he determined to proceed to Ougein. King Bhoja treated him with all respect, and called an assembly of all his five hundred learned men, Kálidás, Kridachandra, Bhavabhúti, and the rest, to dispute with him. They were entirely defeated by the Southern Pandit. Next day King Bhoja, greatly chagrined, went out to take exercise, and on his way he saw a certain oilman, called Ganga, blind of an eye, throwing the oil-seed into the oil-press. "What a wise man must this be," said he to himself, "if the saying be true, 'that a dwarf and a man with yellow eyes have sixty tricks, a man born without a leg or an arm has a hundred, but the number that he has who is blind of an eye no one can tell.'" Going up therefore to the oilman, the King asked him, if he would try his skill in disputing with the learned foreigner. The oilman replied, "What can I do, or what reputation for learning have I? yet, come, victory may through haphazard decide in my favour; I will make the experiment." On Sunday next, the King having called the Southern Pandit said to him, "O Bhatta Achárya, you have vanquished all my learned men, it is true, but you have not yet come in contact with their instructor; I wish you to-day to enter the lists with him." "Very well," the

spoke to her as follows;—"O beloved of the gods, it is declared in the Institute of Dreams, that there

---

other replied. Seats were then set for all the wise men of Bhoja's Court, one for the Bhatta Achárya, and a special seat reserved for Ganga, the oilman. After the whole assembly of learned men and courtiers were met, the King ordered Ganga, who had been dressed in the most splendid style, to be introduced. On his entering the King rose up to receive him, and the whole of his Pandits and courtiers followed his example; and now the debate, at the King's order, commenced. The Southern Pandit, on observing Ganga narrowly, said to himself, "This is a fat stout fellow, whereas I am spare and feeble,—possibly he may overpower me by sheer noise and wordy declamation; let me therefore keep to first principles." Accordingly he began by holding up one finger—Bhoja Raja's new Pandit held up two. After reflecting a little, the Southern Pandit stretched out his arm with his five fingers expanded,—Bhoja Raja's Pandit immediately stretched out his arm with his fist clenched. Instantly the Southern Bhatta Achárya came down from his seat, and fell at Ganga's feet, took out the elephant's hook from his turban, loosed the band which was around his loins, burnt his bunch of grass, broke his ladder, knocked the head off the pickaxe, and prepared to return defeated to his own country. "What is all this," said the King, "will you explain it to us?" "O," said the Southern Pandit, "this Pandit of yours is a learned man indeed, a perfect sage; I held up one finger, intimating that there is one Siva (Spirit), he held up two, signifying that Siva was nothing without Sakti (Matter). Next I held out my five fingers, to intimate that there are five senses; he clenched his fist, as much as to say, these five senses must be restrained." Thus crest-fallen he left the assembly. When he was gone, the King asked the oilman what sense he attached to the dumb

are forty common dreams," &c. [*just as the Brahman before had said*]. After this announcement had been made to her, the noble Trisalá unhesitatingly received what had been declared to her, and, having paid the King due reverence with joined hands, took her departure, and went to her own apartments.

From the day that the venerable ascetic Mahávíra took up his abode in the royal family, Kuvera, with all the hosts of earth's inhabiting gods, called Trimbaka, under his command, had orders from Sakra to search every place where treasure was likely to be, and, when they had found any, to carry it to the house of Siddhártha; namely, to search out treasures of which the owners or guardians were dead, and the families to which they belonged had become extinct, or of which the owners or guardians and families to which they belonged had emigrated, and been long absent from the

---

debate carried on between him and the Southern Pandit. "O," said Ganga, "he first held up one finger, twitting me with having only one eye; I held up two, as much as to say, You have two now, but take care that I do not knock out one of them; he then stretched out his hand, as I understood it, threatening to give me a slap on the face: I then in a rage clenched my fist, thus bidding him take care that I did not knock out his teeth." The King and his courtiers, after enjoying a hearty laugh, dismissed the oilman with many presents.

country, whether the treasure were in villages, or cities, or hamlets, clumps of cottages, or sheds, camps, market-towns, hermitages, threshing-floors, islands, places where three roads meet in a point, or where three or four roads cross each other, stands for carriages, spaces before temples, king's highways, waste villages, waste cities, common sewers of villages or cities, in the streets of towns, in temples, in court-houses, in places for drawing water, in pleasure-gardens, parks, forests of one kind, and forests of different kinds of trees, plantations, clumps of trees on mountains, places on mountains for propitiating demons, ruined houses, and every other place where treasure is to be found. Accordingly, from the day that the venerable ascetic Mahávíra entered the family of King Siddhártha, the royal treasures and ornaments of gold greatly increased, coin and grain increased in the country, the inhabitants increased, the strength of the army increased, the infantry, elephants, and chariots, the number of his treasuries and store-rooms, the members of the royal household, the citizens and men of distinction, all increased. In fine, golden ornaments, jewels, pearls, sacred conchs, crystals, corals, rubies, and other precious stones, all increased a hundredfold. The parents of Mahávíra, considering that they had now obtained the boon they had so long wished for, and so long prayed for, determined that, in consideration of the great increase that had taken place in every species of wealth, he should be called The Increaser (Vardhamána*).

---

* This then is the proper name of the last Jain Tirthankár, though Mahávíra (the Hero) has almost entirely supplanted it, in popular usage, like the Africanus and Germanicus of the classics.

CHAPTER V.

THE BIRTH OF MAHÁVÍRA.

SOME time after this the mother of the adorable ascetic Mahávíra was greatly distressed, at finding that since the time of his conception he had never moved, but continued perfectly still, gathering together all his members. "This babe," said she, "must be dead or torpid, or dissolving, that it continues thus motionless;" and cherishing such reflections, she sat down with her cheek leaning on her hand, looking to the ground, and utterly disconsolate. On learning the state of the Queen, a stop was put to singing, playing on the tabour, violin, and tambourine, and to dancing, in the palace of Siddhártha, and all the courtiers went about idle with downcast countenances. Thereon the adorable ascetic Mahávíra having, by an act of intelligence, brought before him what was passing in his mother's mind, moved a little to one side, when Trisalá again resumed her wonted cheerfulness, and all gloom was dissipated. On account of this incident Mahávíra resolved, that in this

Institute no one should be permitted to be shaved, leave his house, and abandon his family, as long as his father and mother were alive.

The noble Trisalá having bathed, and made her offerings to the inferior divinities*, partook daily of articles of food, which were neither cold, nor hot, pungent, bitter, nor astringent, neither sour nor sweet, oily, harsh, unripe, nor parched, eating always what was proper for the season of the year, and not only in food, but also in clothing, scents, and ointments, studying to use such things as should prevent disease, grief, and longings, while at the same time she was on her guard against frights and fatigues. In such circumstances a mother should be careful to use a healthy diet, suited to the country and season. She should sleep on a firm and easy couch, in pleasant apartments, suited to exhilarate the mind, have a place where she can take exercise, and, as a general rule,

---

* We have here in all the copies कयबल्लिकम्मा performed the Bali worship; and as this was done by the mother of a Tirthankár, it is perplexing to those rigid Jains, who condemn this worship. The Brahmans, too, discourage these ceremonies; but among Hindus, Jains, and Buddhists, no rites are more carefully practised than these, which all their priesthoods condemn, shewing that they must belong to an aboriginal form of worship, which prevailed among the people before the introduction of these new religions from the North.

her longings should be gratified. Thus spending her time happily, in sitting, standing, sleeping, reclining, and taking exercise, the period of her confinement arrived, and the child was born. It was in the summer season, in the first month, in the second demi-lunation, during the bright half of the moon of Chaitra, on the thirteenth day, after a gestation of nine months and seven and a half days, that the venerable ascetic Mahávíra was born, a faultless child, when the planets were at their greatest elongation, and when they were in a fortunate conjunction with the moon*, while all the regions were in a state of placidity, while there was no darkness, but all luminous, without any louring redness, and nightingales† singing

---

* This fortunate conjunction of the moon with the planets, so often mentioned, is as follows:—

षट६ सप्त७ रंध्र८ संस्थैर्भौम्यैरिन्दोः शुभोपियोगोयं

That is to say, the fortunate conjunction is, when Mars and the Moon meet in the 6th, 7th, or 9th Lunar Asterism. As to what is said above about the planets being all in their places of greatest elongation, it is probably a mere rhetorical flourish, the planets, according to the Hindu astronomers, having never been in that position since the commencement of the Kali Yuga, B. C. 3102, and the Author had no intention, as will afterwards appear, of throwing back the birth of Mahávíra to that remote era.

† The Syáma (*Turdus macrourus*). The original is सउणेसु

songs of triumph, and the purifying wind moving gently along, and circling around the place where lay the Lord and his mother. The joyous multitude were engaged in celebrating the vernal festival*, and even the earth seemed to share in the delight. It was at midnight, under the constellation Uttara Phálguni, at a lucky conjunction of the moon and planets, that the event took place. On the night in which the adorable ascetic was born, many gods and goddesses continued going and coming to and from this world with a divine splendour, manifesting, by laughter and other signs, the intensity of their joy. On the night in which the adorable ascetic Mahávíra was born, many divinities, dwellers in the world under the command of Kuvera, rained down showers of precious ores, gold, diamonds, garments, jewels, sweet-smelling leaves, of flowers, fruits, seeds, garlands, ambergris, sandal-wood, and strings of pearls. The four classes of gods, those who dwell in subterranean places, those of the aërial regions, those of the starry firmament, and those from the highest heavens, all flocked to the abode of the noble

---

* In the Deccan there is the Máruti Jayanti held at this time, but the great vernal festival is celebrated a month earlier. These festivals are not Brahmanical, but belong to the ancient ritual of the Hindus.

Siddhártha, to hold the high festival of the inauguration of the Tirthankar*.

Early in the morning, the King having called his messengers-at-arms, said to them: "O beloved of the gods, go quickly through the city of Kundagráma, and liberate all the prisoners†, and order all the dealers to increase their weights and measures for the day. Take care also that all the city, both inside and outside, and the gates, be sprinkled with water, and smeared with cow-dung‡, that places of resort, where three or four ways meet, and spaces around temples, be similarly purified, as also the highways and lanes; also erect a large pavilion, adorned with parti-coloured cloth, hung around with flags, attaching festoons to the ceilings, and put finger-marks on § it of the finest white and red Cashmerian sandal-wood, and put down on the floor a jar of sandal wood, and round it a number of smaller pots. Hang up also garlands over all the doors of sweet-smelling fresh flowers, of all the five different colours, gracefully

---

* This is the Abhisheka; none but gods were present on the occasion, or took part in the festival.

† The original phrase for this is, चारगसीहणंकरेह that is, चारागारशोधनंकुरुत as explained बंदिमोचणकुरुत

‡ A common practice now on festive occasions.

§ This is also a common practice.

strung together, and with the garlands falling down in the form of a necklace. Take then black aloe-wood, and other kinds of sweet-smelling incense, and light them, so as to produce wreaths of delightful perfumes, filling the whole place with sweet odours. Order dancers, and pole dancers, wrestlers, boxers, jesters, story-tellers, reciters of poetry, ballad singers, players on cymbals, on tambourines, and on wind and stringed instruments, along with those who toss up poles, and double balls, all to be present, and aid in the rejoicings." Having received the King's commands, the royal messengers*, glad and rejoicing, and making suitable obeisance, went through the city executing the King's orders, and then returned to report that they had fulfilled all his commands. This morning King Siddhártha went to the gymnasium, exercised himself, bathed, and dressed as above narrated. Then, arrayed in his royal robes, accompanied by his guards, and players on all kinds of musical instruments, he stepped into his palanquin of state, and ordered proclamations to be made, as he went through the city, by sound of conchs, drums, tabours, cymbals, and tambourines, that there should be a release of all presents

---

* These are the *Kadambiya* we before met with, and who at the commencement of this paragraph are in the original mentioned by words that mean as translated—Messengers-at-Arms.

of cloth, and of all customs, of taxes on cattle, and husbandry, and other taxes, that no arrests should be made, that small fines should be remitted, and larger reduced one-half, and debts cancelled, and that dances, plays, and all kinds of music provided for the people, and the city give itself to joy and festivity for ten days. During these ten days of festivity Siddhártha received hundreds and thousands, and tens of thousands of gifts, and gave and ordered to be distributed among his servants, hundreds, and thousands, and tens of thousands of donations. The first day there was performed the feast of special rejoicing for the birth of a son*, the third day was the shewing him the moon, and the sun†; on the sixth day was observed the religious wake‡; the eleventh day put an end to the

---

* In Sanskrit called स्थितिप्रतीचा

† The Commentator says, that instead of shewing the child the actual sun and moon, they form a golden or brass image of the former, and a silver one of the latter, and shew it these.

‡ The mother and her attendants keep awake all this night from respect, my informants say, to the Goddess *Sati,* or as the Marathas call her, Satvâi, who comes to write the child's fate in its forehead. The lines formed for the blood-vessels inside the skull, and especially the serrated lines of the junction of the frontal and parietal bones, are supposed by the Hindus to be the work of a deity, and to contain a record of a man's fate. Accordingly, in the Deccan for "fated," they use the expression, "written on the forehead."

uncleanness incident to the mother on the birth of a son; and accordingly, on the twelfth day, all kinds of articles for eating and drinking, along with sweetmeats and digestives, were prepared for friends, relatives, fathers and mothers-in-law, dependants, and multitudes of the Kshatriya caste, who were invited to the feast. Trisalá, therefore, having bathed, and worshipped the inferior gods, and performed those ceremonies required to prevent misfortune; clothed the child in pure, auspicious, fine, light, valuable raiment, and adorned it with jewels; she then gave it rice to eat, and put it into an easy cradle. After which, the abovementioned parties sat down to enjoy the feast prepared for them. After dinner was finished, and the mouth ablution was performed, and the place made perfectly clean,—the guests were adorned with flowers, and garlands, and scented robes, and jewels, when the noble Siddhártha thus addressed them:—"O beloved of the gods, shortly after the time of my child's conception, on account of the increase that took place in my treasures, and every thing relating to the kingdom, I resolved, that as soon as the child was born, he should be called Vardhamána (The Increaser)—the desire of my heart having been accomplished, I now impose upon him that name. He also is called Sramana, Bhagavan, Mahávíra (The Ascetic, Adorable, Hero). The name Sramana is given because he is devoid of fear and terror, and insensible to all the ills of life, both natural and incidental, possessed of a mind calm and patient under injuries, imbued with true wisdom, and insensible to pain or pleasure. He is called Mahávíra because he conquers the passions, and thus shews himself possessed of true heroism; and he is named Bhagaván because he is worthy of divine honours." The father of the Ascetic Lord had also three names, Siddhártha, Sriyánsa, Yasasvi; and his mother also, who was called Trisalá, Videhadinná, Pritikárani. His eldest paternal uncle was named Supársva, and his eldest brother Nandivarddhana, and his sister Sudarsani. His wife was named Yasodá. He had a daughter who had two names, Sesházvati and Yusovati.

CHAPTER VI.

MAHÁVÍRA'S PUBLIC LIFE AND DEATH.

THE venerable ascetic Mahávíra was learned and intent on the acquisition of knowledge, perfect in his form, and free from all defects, benevolent and affable in disposition, of distinguished rank, the son of a man distinguished in rank, and himself like the moon (among the stars) in his illustrious family; his body was perfectly symmetrical, the son of a symmetrical mother, and the most symmetrical of his family*. Thirty years he lived as a householder, but after the departure to the abode of the gods of his father and mother, he determined to carry out his purpose, and obtained the consent of his brother, who had now become king. At that time, also, the gods who attend on Jina saluted him, and announced to him that the period for becoming an ascetic had arrived, in these words: "Victory, victory to thee! O Chief of the

* There is a play on the word Videhi here used. See above.

Kshatriyas, lay to heart our words; O Lord, ruler of the people, promote the world's happiness, become the sanctuary of religion*, and in the whole world, to every living creature become the author of prosperity, felicity, and future bliss." On finishing, they made the sound of victory to resound through the atmosphere. While the venerable ascetic Mahávíra was yet living in the society of men, and following the religious practice of a householder, he had obtained incomparable, all manifesting, indestructible intelligence and perception†. Therefore, by this incomparable, all-manifesting intelligence and perception, clearly seeing that the time of his initiation had arrived, he abandoned in fixed resolve all his silver, abandoned all his gold, his wealth, kingdom, country, army, chariots, treasury, store-houses, city, private apartments, and society; and taking his money, golden ornaments, jewels, precious stones, pearls, conchs, corals, rubies, and other precious stones, he distributed them in charity, and divided them among his relations. All this happened in the winter season, the first month, the first half of the

---

* धर्मतीर्थ in allusion probably to तीर्थंकर

† अणुत्तरे आहोई अप्पडिवाई नाणदंसणेहोथा This was not yet, however, the highest grade, as will afterwards appear.

month, that is to say, after the full moon of Márgashirsha, the tenth day, when the shadow was turned to the east, and but one watch of the day remained, on the day called Obeisance (Sannati), and the hour (Muhúrta) called Victory (Vijayenam). Then in the palanquin of state, called Lunar Radiance (Chandra Prabhá), he proceeded, accompanied by gods, men, and Titans, bearing, some conchs, some quoits, and some golden ploughshares; some acted the part of heralds, some raised the weak to see the show, some personated bards*, some sounded gongs, and all, in melodious accents, spoke as follows:—"Victory, victory, and prosperity! Victory, victory to thee! O Lord, possessed of indestructible intelligence and perception, conqueror of the unconquered passions, protector of the Ascetic Religion†! O thou, who hast for ever overcome every obstacle, O divine sage, who art now united to perfection, bind the two giants,

---

* Here we have first the मुहमंगलिय probably the officers who precede great men to proclaim their titles, as is still the custom; next we have वद्धमाणा which, in the Sanskrit translation is स्कंधारोपितपुरुषाः and which in the Gujaráthi is said to be men lifted on the shoulders of others; next we have पूसमाणा translated पुष्पमाणाः or मागधाः bards.

† समणधम्म the Jain sages' religion.

Anger and Malice, by thy austerities, and, like a hero, girding up thy loins, overcome the eight enemies whose power lies in works, and performing the purest and chief kind of meditation, devoid of passion, like a warrior seize the flag of victory erected in the battle-field of the three worlds, and obtain a knowledge cloudless, incomparable, perfect and supreme, rise to emancipation, the highest state of bliss*, by that most excellent of roads pointed out by the Jinas, a road free from all perplexing deviousness, and slay all the foes that oppose thy progress. Victory! victory to the Chief of the Kshatriyas, for many days, many fortnights, many months, many seasons, many holy years, many years; having vanquished all natural evils, and accidental diseases, may he obtain perfect patience and equanimity, subduing fear and grief, and performing without obstruction every required religious act." So saying, they again made the air resound with the shout of "Victory! victory!" Thereon the adorable ascetic Mahávíra, gazed on by a circle of thousands of eyes, praised by a circle of thousands of mouths, venerated by a circle of thousands of hearts, surrounded by a circle

---

* It is worthy of notice here that the highest state of bliss परमं पदं is said to be सुखं (Moksha), shewing that the Jains consider Nirvána and Moksha the same.

of thousands whose hearts were won to religion by his conduct, pointed out with admiration by the right hand fore-fingers of a circle of thousands of men and women, with a circle of thousands of joined hands raised in reverence, with a circle of thousands of friends and relations taking leave of him, and with the sound of violins, drums, cymbals, tambourines, and other instruments of music, and a chorus of voices, shouting "Victory, victory!" accompanied also with all his wealth, all his glory, all his troops, all his chariots, all his attendants, all his magnificence, all his ornaments, all his grandeur, all his wealth, all his subjects, all his dancers, all his musicians, all the members of the female apartments, in the midst of all these attendants, and while all those musical instruments were sounding, he proceeded through the midst of Kundanagar, to the garden called the Prince's Park, where the Asoka (Free from Sorrow) tree grew; under it he alighted from his palanquin of state, and stripped himself of all his garlands, jewels, and ornaments; he then performed the fast of abstinence from six meals without drinking water*, and having torn out five locks of his hair, he then,

* The Jains take two meals daily like other Hindus; this fast then, is a fast continued through two whole days and during the afternoon of the preceding and forenoon of the succeeding day.

under the constellation Uttara Phálguna, at a fortunate conjunction of the moon, assumed the garment of the gods*, and all alone, without a companion, and having been shaved, from a householder he became a houseless pilgrim. The adorable ascetic hero for one year and a month wore clothing, afterwards he went robeless†, and had no vessel but his hand. The adorable ascetic Mahávíra, for twelve years and full six months, entirely neglected his body, and laid aside all care of his person, and with whatever things he was brought in contact, whether gods, men, or other animals, whether pleasing or displeasing, he conducted himself with perfect patience and equanimity, and felt nothing dispirited by the wretchedness of his condition. The adorable ascetic Mahávíra was

* The Commentator says this was a robe given him by Indra; perhaps it was the small piece of cloth the Hindus never take off, called a Lunguti, but it is clear that the Jains do not understand properly what it means, or do not wish to explain it. It might have meant he became a Digambara, had this not been opposed to what follows.

† Achelâe. The Commentator introduces a ridiculous story about a Brahman begging his garment, and Mahávíra's giving it him, as the cause of his being naked; he forgets also that he had explained Achelaka to mean with little clothing, instead of having none, so contrary to nature is this practice of the two chief Tirthankars, intended no doubt to show their entire superiority to all passion.

now houseless, a wanderer, a speaker of the truth, eating only what had no fault, having no vessel either to receive presents, or to make oblations, (to the gods or manes)*, regardless of the rules prescribed about natural evacuations, phlegm, and the scurf of the skin, indifferent about gratification from his mind, his speech, or his body, restraining the mind, the speech, and the body, sensual appetite, anger, courtesy, affection, and desire; altogether free from pride, perturbation, sin, and selfishness, having no gold, plate, nor coin; and as water does not enter the substance of the brazen vessel that is dipped into it, nor sound into that of the conch which emits it, so his soul was not subject to the accidents of mortality, but like the firmament, raised above the world, unrestrained like air and fire, and pure as the showers in spring. He was perfect in beauty like the lotus leaves, like the tortoise he had restrained all his corporeal organs, he was single and alone, like the horn of the rhinoceros, like a bird not easily caught, like the eagle, never off his guard, strong as an elephant, patient as a bullock under his

---

* The original is आयाणभंडमत्तनिखेवणसमिए the last word in Sanskrit is सम्यग्मति and properly means indifferent, though the force of it comes to be, regardless, as afterwards once translated.

load, like the lion difficult to be restrained, stable as Mount Mandara, deep as the ocean, mild as the moon, and refulgent as the sun. His person resembled pure gold, and was of the colour of pure honey or fire; and yet he was patient as the earth, trodden on by the feet of all the world—he had no attachment or tie binding him to the world. These ties are of four kinds: articles of possession, place, time, affections. The first consists partly of animate, partly of inanimate objects. Place is either villages, cities, forests, fields, threshing-floors, houses, courts, or heavenly mansions. Times are instants (avali), moments (anu), breathings (prana), thavas (stoka), kohanas, lavas, muhúrtas, days, fortnights, months, seasons, half-years, years, and ages*. Affections are anger, humility, deceit, desire, fear, joy, love, hatred, sorrow, slandering, misjudging, anxiety, doting affections, falsehood, false alarms. None of these things affected the Lord Mahávíra.

On finishing the rest of the rainy season, the venerable ascetic Mahávíra travelled eight months, during hot and cold weather, remaining a night at a village, and five in a city, esteeming the dust of

---

* 167 77, 216 moments = 1 prána, 7 breathings = 1 thava, 6 thavas = 1 muhúrta, 77 lavas = ditto. The muhúrta is, as among the Brahmans, the $\frac{1}{30}$ of a day and night.

ill-flavoured wood and of sandal-wood the same; looking on grass and pearls, gold and a clod of earth, pleasure and pain as all alike, bound neither to this world nor to the world to come, desiring neither life nor death, wholly superior to worldly attachments, setting himself to slay the enemy, Works. Thus did he labour for twelve years in the road that leads to absolute repose (Nirvána), to attain perfect wisdom and perception, religious practice, abstraction from the love of home and country, power, indifference to every object, readiness to obey, patience, freedom from desire, self-restraint, joy, truth, mercy and perfection in austerity. In the second half of the thirteenth year, when half a month had elapsed in the summer season, in the second month of summer, the month Vaisákha, in the fourth demilunation, the tenth day after the full moon, when the shadow was going eastward, and one watch remained on the day called Savita, and the Muhúrta called Vijaya, at the town of Trímbhikagráma, outside the town, at a river called Rituválika, at a moderate distance from a Yaksas temple, called Vairyavartta, in the field of a husbandman named Sáma, under a Sála-tree, sitting in a crouching posture as one does in milking a cow, while inflaming his mind with devotion on the heated earth, and after the fast of six meals without the use of water, under the constellation Uttara Phálguni, at the time of a fortunate lunar conjunction, while he was engaged in abstract meditation, he obtained infinite, incomparable, indestructible, unclouded, universal, perfect, certain, supreme intelligence and perception*. Thereupon the adorable ascetic hero having become an Arhat, (worthy of divine honours,) a Jina, (a conqueror of the passions,) a man of established wisdom, omniscient, all-percipient, he knew and saw all the qualities of the three worlds inhabited by gods, men, and demons, being perfectly acquainted with all the comings and goings, standings and movements of all living creatures, in all worlds, as well as with their mental cogitations, lawful and unlawful enjoyments†, and their open and concealed actions; being an Araha, (one from whom nothing is concealed,) and the undisguised object of worship to all beings. At that time, then, having obtained a perfect knowledge and perception of all the qualities and conditions of all living creatures, in all the world, characterized by mental, vocal, or bodily attributes, he continued ever after to enjoy the same.

---

* The original here is अणंते अणुत्तरे निव्वाघाए निरावरणे कसिणे केवलवरनाणदंसणा समुप्पन्ने describing an omniscience the most complete, and nothing short of perfect deification.

† A paraphrase of भुत्तकंडपडिसेविय

At this time the adorable ascetic Mahávíra came to the town of Asthigráma, and spent there the first rest of the rainy season. Proceeding then to Champa and Prishtachampa he there spent three, at Vánijyagráma near Vaisáli he spent twelve, and in the village of Nalinda near Rajagriha fourteen, six at Mithilá, two at Bhadrika, one at Alambhika, one at Srávasti, one at Panitabhúmi, and the last rest of the rainy season he spent at Pápa, where reigned King Shastipála. There having spent the season of rest at the royal court, in the fourth month, in the seventh demilunation, on the night immediately preceding the new moon, was the time of the adorable ascetic hero completed, his earthly career finished, the bands of decay and death loosed, and he entered on a state of perfect bliss, wisdom, liberty, freedom from care and passion, and absence of all pain*. This took place in the second year named Chandra, in the month Pritivardhana, in the demilunation Nandivardhana, in the day named Agnivesha, and surnamed Upa-

---

* These attributes of the state of Nirván are surely inconsistent with annihilation; सिद्ध बुद्धे मुत्ते अंतगडे परिंनिव्वुडे सव्वदुखपहिणे the fifth translated "freedom from passion;" in *Sans.* सर्वसंतापाभावात् is the one that denotes Nirván properly.

sáma, in the night named Devanandá, and surnamed Nirati, at the Lava named Archa, the Muhúrta called Prâna, the Stoka named Siddhi, the Karana called Nága, at the astrological period named Sarvártha-siddhi, in the constellation Sváti, at the time of its conjunction with the moon. At that time many gods and goddesses were seen in heavenly splendour, ascending and descending through the aërial regions, and manifesting themselves by the whispering sounds they uttered. On the night on which the adorable ascetic hero was delivered from all pain, Gotama Indrabhúti, the chief of his perfectly initiated disciples, had the bonds of affection by which he was tied to his preceptor cut asunder, and attained infinite, certain, and supreme intelligence and perception. On the same night the Navamallika and Navalechhiki, kings who reigned at Kási and Kosala, after performing the fast of the new moon, and sitting awhile motionless, said, "Since the light of intelligence is gone, let us make an illumination of material substances." On the same night the planet Kshudra Bhasmaka*, destined to continue two thousand years, ascending the natal constellation

---

* *Mag.* Khuddae Ahasarasi. *Sans.* Krúrasvábhavabhasma rási. The test is the Gujarathi paraphrase, and probably refers to the appearance at the time of a comet, called here ग्रह.

of the Lord Mahávíra, and as long as it continues there, there will be a great waning of piety and religious worship, among male and female ascetics and religious persons, but when the planet descends from that constellation, ascetism and piety will blaze forth with new brilliance. On the same night an animal called the *Imprehensible*, was produced, and continued fixed in one place, producing in ascetics a want of distinct vision. On seeing this many male and female ascetics performed the fast of abstinence from food and water. (The disciple inquires) Why was the animal produced, my Lord? It was to shew that the observance of the religious institute would now be difficult.

At the time and season mentioned the adorable ascetic Mahávíra had, with Gotama Indrabhúti at their head, an excellent select band of fourteen thousand male ascetics; and with Chandrabalá at their head, an excellent select band of thirty-six thousand female ascetics; with Sankhasataka at their head an excellent select band of one hundred and fifty-nine thousand male lay adherents; and with Salasá-revati at their head, an excellent select band of three hundred and eighteen thousand female lay adherents. The adorable ascetic hero had three hundred and fourteen advanced disciples, possessed of a wisdom next to perfect, and knowing theoretically all that a Jina knows, without being perfect Jinas*, and of these fourteen were superior to the rest. He had a band of thirteen hundred disciples, possessed of inductive knowledge, seven hundred possessed of certain knowledge, seven hundred possessed of the power of assuming a different form, and though not gods had the power of gods; five hundred of large intellect, acquainted with all the thoughts and feelings of all sentient beings, in two and a half continents and two seas†; a company of four hundred disputants that had never been overcome in any assembly of gods, asurs, or men. He had seven hundred male disciples, who on dying obtained perfect liberation, and fourteen female. He had two hundred and fifty who obtained that super-celestial mansion, from which beings only once descend to mortal birth before obtaining liberation. The venerable ascetic hero instituted two peculiar world-vanquishing periods, one unlimited except by the Yuga, and the other embracing a limited time. The former extended to three disciples in succession, and the latter continued

---

* The original is अजिणाणं जिणसंकासं सव्वाखरसन्निवादूणं in Sanskrit अजिनापि जिनसदृशाः सर्वाक्षरसमूहज्ञातारः

† Namely in Jambudvipa, Dhátuki Khanda and Urdha Pushkar, and the salt and fresh-water sea, all our earth.

only four years*. The venerable ascetic Mahávíra lived thirty years as a householder, and then twelve years and six months and a full half month more a sage only in outward guise†; thirty years less six and a holy month in the exercise of perfect wisdom, altogether having lived seventy-two years. At that time the four Karans of this Avasarpiní, *i. e.* Vedani, Ayu, Náma, and Gotra, were finished, and the fourth Ara, called Dukhamasukhama, had all expired except three years, and eight and a half months, in the city of Pápa (Mag. Páwa), alone without a companion, performing the fast in which abstinence is kept up for three full days and nights, without even tasting water, under the constellation Sváti, at a fortunate conjunction of the moon, in the morning, the lord sat down upon his lotus seat, while the public reading of the fifty-fifth lesson, which speaks of the fruits of righteousness and of sin, was going on. At that time repeating without a prompter the sixty-sixth, called the chief lesson, he obtained emancipation, and entered on a state of freedom from passion, and absence of pain. After nine hundred years from his departure had elapsed, and in the eightieth year of the

---

* These refer to peculiar spiritual privileges possessed by certain disciples for this period.

† Chhadmastha, that is, an ascetic, not yet possessed of perfect knowledge.

currency of the tenth hundred, this book was written, and was publicly read in the currency of the ninety-third year*.

---

* It is added in the Gujarathi, at the time of a famine in the city of Mathura. The era is that of Mahávíra, preceding the Samvat of Vikrama, according to the Jains of Gujarath, by 470 years, consequently for the time before the Christian era by adding 56, we get 526, and for the date of the book A. D. 454, and the public reading A. D. 466. The era given as that of Mahávíra in Prinsep's Useful Tables, Indian Chronology, p. 33, is 42 years earlier, corresponding to the time here given for Mahávíra's becoming an ascetic. See Preface, where reasons are given for preferring Mr. Prinsep's date. The date here given is one founded on the mistake of the abandonment of the world for death.

CHAPTER VII.

THE HISTORIES OF PÁRSVA, NEMI, AND RISHABA*.

PÁRSVA, the chief of Arhats, was son of King Asvasena, and of his queen Váma, and was born at Varánasi (Benares), in the second month of winter, the tenth day of Pausha. He adopted an ascetic life, with three hundred others, when he was thirty years of age, and for eighty days he practised austeries, before arriving at perfect wisdom. He lived after this seventy years, less eighty days, his whole term of life being one hundred years, after which he obtained liberation from passion, and freedom from pain. He wore one garment, and had under his direction a large

* These histories are given with a great deal of prolixity, generally in the very words in which Mahávíra's life is detailed. I have therefore confined myself to the few particulars in which they really differ, and in this I have but carried out a little further the plan of the original; for after a few details, जाव is usually added to denote that the other particulars are to be taken from the previous histories.

number of male and female ascetics, and lay disciples. His death took place twelve hundred and thirty years before the composition of this work (*i. e.* B.C. 828). He died while with thirty others performing a fast on the top of Mount Sameta (Sikhar). He is also called Pársvanátha.

The Arhat Nemi was son of King Samudravijaya and his queen Sívá, and was born in the city of Sori (Agra). He was born in Srávan the first month of the rainy season, under the constellation Chitra. He became an ascetic at the age of three hundred at Dváraka (*Mag.* Baravavâe). He died on Mount Girnár, after living seven hundred years as an ascetic, in all a thousand years. He was only fifty-five days an imperfect ascetic. This book was composed eighty-four thousand nine hundred and fifty years after his death*. He is also called Arishta Nemi, and Neminátha.

Rishabha, the Arhat of Kosala, was the son of Nâbhi, and his queen Marudevi. He was born on the eighth day of the waning moon of Chaitra; his mother dreamt of his birth as in the case of other Tirthankars, but saw the bull (Vrishabha) first, and instead of calling a Brahman to interpret particularly her dreams, Nábhi performed that

* Whatever may be said of the date of Mahávíra's life, the author now undoubtedly runs wild. His dates are purely imaginary henceforward, and some are not found in all the copies.

office himself. Rishabha was the first king, the first mendicant, the first Jina, and the first Tirthankar. He spent two hundred thousand years, in the state of youth, reigned six hundred and thirty thousand; for one thousand years he remained an ascetic imperfectly enlightened; in all he lived eight hundred and forty thousand years*.

---

* In some copies there are similar extravagant histories of all the Tirthankars, but not in the best manuscripts. I am inclined to think that the original work ended with the life of Maḥávíra. The Annotator in his Preface speaks only of the times of Mahávíra and Rishabha; and even the latter would seem added by a modern hand, unless it be that unrestrained by traditions transmitted to posterity, of the age and actions of the first Tirthankar, the author indulged his fancy in a way that he durst not do with the more recent sage. The few particulars we have of the other Tirthankars are most likely mere fictions, founded on no solid traditions. The only three historical characters I conceive to be, Rishabha, who practised austerities in very ancient times, which the Jains in after ages imitated; Pársvanáth, the real founder of the Sect, and Mahávíra, who carried its principles out to their utmost limits.

STHIRAVALI.

A LIST OF STHAVIRAS, HEADS OF THE JAIN SCHOOL AFTER MAHAVIRA.

	Name.	Family.	Death after Mahávíra.
1	Sudharma	Vaisya	20 years.
2	Jamba	Kásyapa	64 „
3	Prabhava	Kátyáyana	75 „
4	Sishvambhava	Vátsya	98 „
5	Yasobhadra	Tungiyáyana	146 „
6	Sambhútivijaya	Madara	156 „
	Bhadrabáhu	Práchína	
7	Sthúlabhadra	Gautama	170 „
8	Suhasti	Vasishta	
	Mahágiri	Elavarchasa	215 „
9	Susthita	Kotika	
	Supritibhadra	Vyághrapadya	
10	Indradinna	Kausika	
11	Dinna	Gautama	
12	Sinhagiri	Kausika	
13	Játísvara	Kausika	
14	Vajrasena	Kausika	

	Name.	
15	Nágila	Each of whom was the founder of a Sákhá, or branch called by his own name.
	Padmila	
	Jayanti...............	
	Tapasa	

The succession from the second Teacher of No. 8, the other list being the succession from the first of the same number. (The dates being contained only in the MS. which gives this succession, were not appended to the succeeding numbers above, but are here resumed):—

9	Balisaha	241	19	Sinhasvámi ...	814
10	Sànti...........	280	20	Sándilasvámi .	848
11	Somácharya...	232	21	Hemavanta ...	875
12	Skandila	378	22	Nágárjuna ...	887
13	Jinádhara......	454	23	Govindasvámi.	914
14	Samudrasvámi.	508	24	Bhútidinna ...	942
15	Mangu Svámi.	591	25	Lohitasvámi...	975
16	Nádila Svámi .	684	26	Duppajana ...	988
17	Nágahasti ...	719	27	Kshamasvámi .	993
18	Revatya	790			

N.B. The above list proceeds a generation lower down than the time of the composition of the work, but the author might have added the last name before his death. We have now numerous lists, according to the different branches of the sect, continued till near the present time. One of these is here added:—

15 Chandra.
16 Sámanta Bhadra.
17 Vriddhadeva.
18 Pradyotana.
19 Mána.
20 Mánatunga.
21 Víra.
22 Jayadeva.
23 Devananda.
24 Vikrama.
25 Narasinha.
26 Samudra.
27 Mánadeva.
28 Vibudhaprabha.
29 Jayananda.
30 Raviprabha.
31 Yasodeva.
32 Pradyumna.
33 Srimán.
34 Vimalachhand.
35 Udyota.
36 Sámadeva.
37 Srideva.
38 Yasobhadra.
39 Nemichandra.
40 Radanapura.
41 Munichandra.
42 Ajitadeva.
43 Vijayasinha.
44 Somaprabha.
45 Jagatchandra.
46 Devendra.
47 Dharmagosha.
48 Somatilaka.
49 Devasundara.
50 Somasundara.
51 Manisundara.
52 Ratnasesha.
53 Lakshmiságara.
54 Sumatisádhu.
55 Hemavimala.
56 Anandavimala.
57 Vijayadána.
58 Hira—lived in Akbar's time, A. D. 1556.
59 Vijayasena.
60 Vijayatilaka.
61 Vijayánanda.
62 Vijayarája.
63 Mána.
64 Udvi.
65 Saubhágya.
66 Vijayaudaya.
67 Vijayalakshmi.
68 Vijayadevendra.
69 Vijayamahendra.
70 Vijayasamudra.

THE SAMÁCHÁRIS.

1*st Samáchári.* At that time and season the adorable ascetic Mahávíra commanded that, reckoning from the full moon of Ashádh a month and twenty days, a period of rest and fasting should be observed yearly in the four months of the rainy season*. When the reason of this was asked, he replied that it was intended, first to lead the householder to whiten and thatch his house, smear and clean the walls inside, repair his fence, level and clean his floors, perfume his house, clear the pipes and gutters, that the house might be fitted for the true enjoyments of life; and next that such a

* This divides the rainy season into two periods, one of fifty, and one of seventy days; the Svetámbara Jains fast, during the former, and the Digambara during the latter of these periods, as the test is considered ambiguous. The term for this fast is Paryúshana. Its nature will immediately appear, permitting of a fast, varying from that in which but one meal daily is taken, to that in which abstinence of two, three, or more days is volunteered.

season had always been observed by the leaders of the sacred bands of disciples, by the established sages, and by the ascetics of past and present times, and that therefore it was incumbent upon us, and all our teachers and priests, to keep this season of rest and abstinence. The calculation is to be made so as to come within the night of the fifth of the increase of the moon of Bhádrapad, and not to go beyond it.

2. It is commanded that all males and females, keeping the annual fast, should limit their peregrinations to a circuit of five miles, proceeding beyond that no farther than the time the perspiration takes to dry on the hand.

3. Should a deep constantly-flowing river intervene, within that circuit, they are not permitted to cross it, for the purpose of collecting alms, but where there is a river like Airávati at the town of Kunála, where the water is so shallow that while the one foot is in the water the other can be lifted up above it, permission is given to cross it.

4. Any particular member can only partake of refreshment when permitted by the Abbot, or head of the community. The sick should first be fed, and the rest should then eat, giving to others, as well as partaking themselves.

5. During this lenten period, male and female ascetics in health should by no means partake of

the following articles—rice and milk, curds, fresh butter, melted butter, oil, sugar, honey, spirits, and flesh*.

6. Certain sages having asked for direction in the matter, it was laid down as a rule, that in feeding a sick man, you are only to take what food he may not require, if you have the Superior's permission.

7. It was also ruled, that though lawful to ask of a householder what you see in his house for a sick person, you are not to ask what you do not see. And when the reason of this was asked, the reply given was, that if the householder be a man of great devotedness, he may be induced to go and buy what you want, or if not able to do this, even to steal it.

8. It is permitted those who eat only once a day to go out to collect alms only once a day. This, however, does not permit them to go out again for a teacher, a superior, a sick person, or a novice under age. The following rules are also to be observed. The person who fasts one day and on the preceding and succeeding partakes only of one

---

* It seems more strange that these two last should at other times be permitted than now prohibited, and shews that in those ancient times Jain priests, as well as Brahmans, had different principles from those they now entertain.

meal, should take whatever thing to eat or drink he may have received, and wiping clean the outside of the vessel, go home, and put it down on his mat, and partake of it. He who fasts two days at a time, may on the other days leave the convent twice to enter the abodes of householders in quest of provisions*. He who fasts three days at a time may thrice on the intervening days leave home to seek provisions, and he who fasts more than three days may go as often as he pleases.

9. He who eats one day is permitted to use any kind of water; he who fasts wholly one day, and eats one meal on the preceding and succeeding is permitted only to use three kinds of water, that in which a man's hands have been washed, in which flour has been washed, or in which rice has been washed. He who fasts two days at a time must drink only of the three following kinds of water, that in which oil seed, rice, or barley, has been washed. He who abstains three days from all food must also drink only of three kinds of water, viz., that in which grain has been boiled, water skimmed from butter-milk, and hot water. And he who abstains more days, must drink only hot water; cold water is prohibited. At the same time the

---

* The general rule in all these cases is, that the provisions are cooked, ready for eating, and that the ascetic asks nothing, but takes what is given.

water must be strained; unstrained water is entirely prohibited. It is to be used according to measure also, and taken in limited quantities, even although thirst is not thereby quenched.

10. The ascetic may receive from householders to the extent of four solid and five liquid articles of diet, or five solid and four liquid, and among these as much salt as will season his provisions. But he is only to take for that day's consumption, he is not to go out in search of provisions a second time.

11. Ascetics during the lenten season are not permitted to enter a house till they have passed seven from that of their usual abode. Opinions vary as to whether cottages and such like are to be reckoned among the seven or not.

12. Ascetics who receive cooked food in the hand, are prohibited from going out in quest of alms while it rains, whether the rain be heavy or light. An ascetic who has received food, and consumed a part of it abroad, is not permitted to continue his meal if it begins to rain, but he must cover up with his one hand the food he holds in the other, and retire to a shed or cave*, or the root of a tree,

* The original here is Lena; the *Sans.* is लयनं and उपाश्रयं Lena is the name still given to the caves in which Buddhist and other sacred relics or images are found. Perhaps the best translation here would be Hermitage.

where there is no dropping or drizzling of rain, and there finish his meal.

13. An ascetic who receives cooked food in a vessel must not go out in heavy rain*, but if it rains lightly he may take a cloak and go. If after departure it begins to thunder and lighten, or rain heavily, he should take refuge in a house or convent, or at the root of a tree. He is to take only a share of the cooked victuals removed from the fire before his entrance. If the pulse alone were removed, he is to take only of that. If the rice alone he is to take a share only of the rice; he is prohibited from taking anything that is in a vessel removed from the fire after his entrance. If overtaken in a storm, after receiving a supply of provisions, he may take shelter as aforesaid, but he is not there to eat his meal, only if it is getting late may he eat it, and then clean his vessel, and return home, for he is absolutely prohibited from remaining abroad during the night. Again in retiring for shelter during a storm, one male and one female may not stay in the same place, nor two males and one female, nor two males and two females, nor less than five be together. Nor must a male ascetic who has gone into a house to pro-

---

* Heavy is what will penetrate through a cloak, a country blanket, or kambali.

cure a meal stay there, if there is but one female in the house, or in any of the above-mentioned cases; only when there are five persons together may he remain; but these may be either householders or ascetics. If the place where he stands is open to the street, and to public inspection, he may stay.

14. Ascetics are not to dine or take any article of food without first obtaining leave of the superior. The reason is that he knows their constitution, and what they require best. They are to address him respectfully, saying, "We wish to dine if it be your pleasure, otherwise we will abstain from doing so."

15. No one is to dine while the body is bedewed with water. Water is apt to lodge in the lines of the hands, about the points of the nails, the eyebrows, and the upper and lower lips; the body to be perfectly dried before partaking of a meal.

16. The imperfectly enlightened ascetic* must be on his guard, and carefully look that he do not come in contact with any of the eight small things —small animals, small flowers of mosses and

* Chhadmastha, he who has not yet arrived at perfect knowledge; to the omniscient sage such attention is quite unnecessary. He knows without being on the watch.

grasses, small weeds, small vegetables, small blossoms of shrubs and trees, small eggs, small places, small liquid productions.

Small animals are caterpillars, and the larvæ of animals of blue, black, red, yellow, and white colours. Small flowers and vegetables and blossoms are those respectively of all the five original colours as above. Small eggs are those of the bug and flea kind, the spider kind, the ant kind, the wasp kind, and the lizard kind. Small places are lairs, dens, ant-holes, white ant-hills, and bee-hives. Small liquid productions are dew, hoar-frost, fogs, hail, flakes of snow*. Of all these the imperfectly-enlightened sage must constantly be on his guard.

17. The ascetics are prohibited from going out to collect alms, without first asking the abbot, teacher, established sage, the head of their class, or the person under whose charge they may be. They are thus to address him—"If it be your pleasure we wish to go abroad and obtain articles for eating and drinking, but if you disapprove we will remain at home." The reason of this is, that the superior

---

* The original is, हरतणु and the Sanskrit paraphrase is भूमीनिस्टतत्वणाग्रबिंदुरूपा I am not sure I have hit the exact idea.

best knows the state of the place, the constitutions of the persons, and what other matters require attention. After he has collected his dinner he is also to ask leave before he partake of it. In like manner he is to ask permission before taking medicine. He should also ask before performing any religious rite, or entering on any course of austerities. Nor especially is the ascetic who keeps the lenten rest permitted without leave of the superior to enter on the performance of the Sauleshana rite, in which while absorbed in meditation, and neither eating nor drinking, he comes to the last stage of his earthly pilgrimage, like a tree dropping its leaves in the proper season, wholly unconscious of the fact. It is also prohibited without such leave, to go out for sweetmeats and digestives, or to read the sacred books, or to watch during the night for the performance of religious duties.

18. It is not permitted any one, whether singly or in company with another, to go out to get clothes, a vessel, a blanket, shoes, or any article of clothing, to protect him from the sun or weather, without first obtaining leave to do so, nor to go out, whether to ask alms of householders, or for recreation, or to visit the temples of the sages, or for the necessities of nature, or for meditation. As the superior alone knows the proper season for all things, every one must first respectfully address

him, and having obtained his leave, then go abroad.

19. It is prohibited to any male or female ascetic to be without a couch to sleep on. If they have no bed to sleep on, or if it be too high or too low, if not rightly put together, if not of proper dimensions, if heavy and difficult to move, if not frequently wiped and kept clean, it will be difficult to keep from killing small insects, and so violating the duties of humanity. On the contrary, if possessed of the opposite qualities, it will be easy to perform the duties of humanity.

20. Ascetics are ordered to clean and prepare three different places at a distance from their usual abode, for the three natural excretions. This is not needed in the hot and cold season, but it is required in the rainy season, on account of the multitude of insects, seeds, flowers, &c., which are there produced.

21. Ascetics are ordered to restrain emitting phlegm, or voiding either of the other two natural excretions*, (except in the above-mentioned places).

---

* These, of course, are पुरीष and मूत्र in Mágadhi, उच्चार and पासवण and delicately expressed in Gujarathi by वडीनीति and लघुनीति.

22. It is prohibited to an ascetic to wear hair longer than that which covers a cow. The night of the commencement of the fast must not pass before the ascetic has shaved his head. It should afterwards be shaven monthly, otherwise cut with scissors every fortnight, and shaved at the end of six months, or at any rate, at the end of a year.

23. It is prohibited during the fast to use any angry or provoking language. He or she who does so is not to be allowed to remain in the community.

24. If on account of words that have passed between parties, a quarrel arise, mutual forgiveness is to be asked and granted, the elder disciple is to ask forgiveness of the younger, and the younger of the elder. Self-restraint is also to be exercised by each individually, and the exercise pressed upon others. Those who practise self-control are to be venerated, those who do not are not to be venerated. Self-control is the chief of all religious exercises.

25. Three different cleanings are enjoined of ascetics—the morning picking up of impurities, the midday sweeping, and the evening washing*.

26. Ascetics when going in quest of provisions

* This translation is according to the letter. It may perhaps only mean that there are to be three daily cleanings of the place of these three kinds.

are enjoined to ask the superior whether they are to go to a distance or remain near. The reason of this being, that certain sages on account of the practice of austerities are not fit to go far, and therefore the superior is the proper person to determine who shall remain near and who go to a distance. A sage is not permitted, after wandering about four or five leagues, to stay at the place at which he has arrived, but must return before night. If unable to do so he must return a certain part of the way and lodge there.

27. Those who observe the aforesaid yearly institute of the sages, according to the rules laid down for this institute, with a sincere purpose following the established ritual, performing the worship directed, and obeying the commands given, will some of them, those especially who have already abandoned the world, become perfect in knowledge, and after the termination of their present lives obtain liberation, and freedom from all pain. Others will obtain the same, after two or three transmigrations, and none will exceed the seventh or eighth.

This institute was ordained by the adorable ascetic Mahávíra at Rajgriha, in the sacred garden (Chaitya) of Gunasila, while surrounded by multitudes of male and female ascetics and lay disciples, as well as gods and goddesses.

NAVA TATVA SUTRA;

OR,

THE NINE PRINCIPLES OF THINGS.

THE following are the nine Principles of things: (1) Animation; (2) Inanimate Matter; (3) Merit; (4) Demerit; (5) Appetite and Passion, and other provocatives to sin; (6) Self-Denial, and other helps to virtue; (7) Means to free the Mind from worldly attachments; (8) Worldly Attachments; (9) Final Deliverance*.

Of the first and second of these there are fourteen varieties; of the third, forty-two; of the

* The original is as follows:—जीवाऽजीवा पुणं पावाऽसव संवरोय निज्जरणा बद्धी मुखोय The Sanskrit equivalents are जीव अजीव पुण्य पाप आश्रव संवर निर्जरा बंध मोच तत्वं

fourth, eighty-two; of the fifth, forty-two; of the sixth, fifty-seven; of the seventh, twelve; of the eighth, four; and of the ninth, nine.

I. Animated beings may be considered under one, two, three, four, five, or six aspects; simply as possessed of life; as vegetables and animals; as male, female, and of neither sex; as men, brutes, demons, and gods; as possessed of one, two, three, four, or five senses; and as having a body of earth, water, fire, wind, wood, or flesh.

The fourteen kinds of animate beings are as follows: First, objects with one sense; which are of two kinds, those that are invisible or seen with difficulty, and those that are easily seen, [these are fire, air, earth, and vegetables]. Secondly, Beings with five senses; some of which have a mind, [as men, gods, demons, fowls, and all animals and fishes that are produced, in the Jain estimation, from parents], and others have no mind, [as beings in the embryo state, and those generated, as the Jains think, by equivocal generation, from phlegm, slime, &c., as some kinds of fishes and serpents]. There are then beings possessed of two senses, (viz., touch and taste, as shellfish), and others having three, (viz., touch, taste and smell, as ants and fleas); and still a third class, with four senses, (wanting only hearing, as flies, bees and scorpions). Each of these seven classes of animals may be complete in all their powers or parts, or incomplete, forming the fourteen distinctions among animated beings*.

The most exalted properties of animated beings are, knowledge, perception, initiation into a religious life, the practice of self-denial, the possession of power, and the employment of means to obtain an end.

The following things sustain life: food, a body, the senses, the power of breathing, the power of speech, and mental power. The first four belong to creatures that have but one sense, the first five to creatures having two, three, and four senses, or five without a mind,—and all the six to the creatures that have a mind. There are ten vital airs concerned in the sustaining of life, one for each of the five senses, one that supports the breathing, one on which the term of life depends, and the three invigorating airs, [one for the mind, a second for the speech, and a third for the bodily frame]. Beings with one, two, three, and four senses, have the first four, six, seven, and eight of these

---

* The original word translated, with a mind, is सन्नि Sanskrit मनः संयुक्ताः The word for complete is पज्जाता Sanskrit पर्य्याप्ताः The additions within brackets are all from the Comment, and so in future, except one or two from oral information.

respectively. Those with five senses, and without a mind, have only nine vital airs*.

The union of these with a body constitutes the state of life, and their disjunction the state of death. Fire, air, earth, and water, are called elements†. Trees and flowers of all kinds are called existents‡. Beings with less than five senses are called respirers§, and the four classes of beings with five senses, (viz., gods, men, brutes, and demons), are called properly animated beings‖.

II. The fourteen distinctions of things without life are: solids, fluids, and airs¶, each of which has three aspects. The whole, a territory, and a district**. Add to these time, and the four distinctions of a body††, the whole body, a region, a member, and an atom, and the number is completed. Inanimate objects are then divisible into four classes, solids, fluids, bodies, and air. Fluids

---

* प्राणा: † सत्ता S. सत्वा:

‡ भूअआ S. भूता: § पाणा S. प्राणा:

‖ जीवा ¶ धम्माऽधम्माऽगासा San. धर्मास्तिकाय: अधर्मास्तिकाय: आकाशास्तिकाय:

** खंधदेसपदेसा Sans. स्कंधदेशप्रदेश:

†† पुग्गल S. पुद्गलास्तिकाय:

form a medium in which motion can be performed, solids are stable, air forms the atmosphere, and body is matter formed for the habitation of a living principle, and has the four divisions named above.

The divisions of time are, samaya, avali, muhúrtta, days, demi-lunations, months, years, ages (palyas), oceans (ságara), utsarpini, and avasarpani. [The first is an infinitesimal part of time], and there are sixteen millions, seven hundred and seventy-seven thousand, two hundred and sixteen (16,777,216) avali in a muhúrtta (forty-eight minutes). The two last are the Jain eras, measuring the time between the creation and destruction of the world, as elsewhere explained].

III. The rewards of merit, and themselves productive of merit, are, birth in a good family, in one of the two conditions of manhood, [manhood directly, or indirectly by being removed to a human womb in the embryo state, as narrated of Mahávíra], the two conditions of godhead [*as before*], the possession of the five senses, and of one of the five bodies. These are, a natural body, (udárika); a supernatural assumed temporarily, (vaikriya); one a cubit long, to go to Mahavidehi, a particular terrestrial continent, to obtain of the Tirthankaras there a solution of doubts, (ahárika); a luminous body (tejasvi) like those of the gods; and any body obtained as the fruit of merit, (kármika); to possess also the bones like adamant, and the perfect form of a Tirthankare, a good colour, smell, taste, touch, and the proper proportion of heaviness, and lightness, inoffensiveness, moderate breathing, a brilliant countenance, elegant motion, and members all properly balanced, the state of a god, that of man, that of the highest classes of animals, and that of a Tirthankar. These, in addition to the following ten modes of action, form the forty-two meritorious states. The modes of action are, voluntary motion, right use of the senses, of all the other organs, a separate body for the soul to act on, firmness in action, pleasantness in deportment, elegant gesture, speaking with a sweet voice, in a persuasive manner, and so as to elicit praise.

IV. The effects and causes of sin are the following:—The ten divisions of want of knowledge, [first of things mental, then of words, then a want of perfect knowledge of sensible objects, the want of knowledge of what is doing in all the forty-five divisions of the world, then in the fifteen the abode of man, next, want of omniscience; besides there is incapacity of giving, inability to obtain the object of desire, incapacity of securing delight, and inability to enjoy]. There are also nine natural infirmities, [imperfection of sight and sleep; of the former four, and of the latter five, viz., total want of sight, incapability of seeing what is not before the eyes, incapability of seeing all that is done on earth, incapability of seeing all things; and sleep, deep sleep, sleep in which one can sit or stand, sleep in which a person can walk about, mesmeric sleep, in which a tooth might be pulled out or a limb cut off without the patient's knowledge, and in which he can exert supernatural strength in accomplishing plans thought of during the day*].

Next there is, birth in a low family, any act that gives pain, false worship, the state of any of the ten kinds of living beings destitute of motion, any of the three states in hell, [descending naturally there, being drawn away to it, and living in it]; being under the influence of any of the twenty-five passions, [sixteen proper, as, anger, pride, love, covetousness, each of four kinds; and things connected with passion, as laughter, &c., six things, and the three sexual states of animals]; the four classes of living beings with one, two, three, and four senses; bad gait; natural defects, [as, a buck-tooth, &c.]; also disagreeable colour, smell, taste, or feel; any one of the five conditions of the bones or form of the body other than that above decribed, under the opposite head: all these are con-

---

* This is called by the Jains Asvápani Nidra, although I cannot learn that they are acquainted with any process by which it is induced.

nected with the principle of sin. Besides, there are want of proper motion in any member of the body, extreme minuteness, improper developement, excessive hairiness, want of firmness; and the following acts, indelicate contact, [touching any part of the body below the navel], causing distress to any being, inharmonious sound, disobedience, disrespect.

V. Appetites and passions, and other incitements to sin. These are the five senses and the four passions, [anger, pride, love, covetousness]; the five sinful acts, [killing, stealing, lying, adultery, devotedness to the world]; the three yogas, [applications of the mind, speech, and body, to worldly objects]; besides the twenty following acts: walking carelessly, [and so endangering the life of insects], lending a weapon, wishing ill to any being, teazing any being or injuring them, beginning any work, [as ploughing], the reception of a gift, the exercise of cunning, accusing the Jain sacred books of falsehood, acting without any rule, seeing stage plays, touching things forbidden, [as horses, bulls, and women, which are prohibited to ascetics]; hearing one's own praises proclaimed, bearing weapons, beating animals, purchasing articles to sell them at a profit, piercing any animal with a weapon, doing things with carelessness, disregard of the good opinion of gods and men, ordering others to do what you should do yourself, mingling in a crowd of people, currying favour with others, cherishing malicious purposes, and travelling, [in which, from liability to tread on small insects, the danger of sinning is incurred].

VI. Self-denial, religious restraint, and other helps to a course of virtuous action. These are, the five cares about externals, the five cares about internals; twenty kinds of patient endurance, and ten kinds of virtuous actions. Of the first named, attention to the road on which you walk, [that there be no insects on it to sustain injury], attention to what you say, and what you eat, care about what you receive, [that you do not put it down on the ground and allow ants to mingle with it, &c.], and care about excretions. Of the second named, or care about internals, there is one care to exclude improper and to introduce religious subjects of meditation, care to cover your mouth when you speak, [lest some fly or animal enter it], and to avoid all kinds of sin. The following things are to be patiently borne: hunger, thirst, cold, heat, the bite of any animal, while you are engaged in religious worship, dirty and ragged clothes, the solicitations of passion, the absence of female society, the inconveniences of travel, the appearance of ghosts, an uncomfortable couch, railing, murderous blows, begging, disappointment in obtaining what we desire, disease, a straw pallet, dirt, honour, the praise of knowledge, the disgrace of ignorance, and religious doubts. The ten acts are as follows: the mildness that restrains wrath, the humility which subdues pride, the simplicity which is opposed to cunning, the spirituality which is opposed to worldly-mindedness, fasting and austerities, self-restraint, speaking the truth, tender regard for the life of all creatures, abandonment of all worldly possessions, celibacy and chastity. These things contain the principles of the Jain religion.

VII. Raising the mind from worldly attachments. To effect this the following nine reflections are to be kept before the mind: that all things are unstable, that death and the ills of life cannot be prevented, that man is driven through a succession of states in different worlds, that the same life is frequently passing through births and deaths, that the body is but a receptacle for filth, that man is through the actions he is called on to perform exposed to innumerable temptations to sin, that these may be resisted, and that works of all kinds should be abstained from. In addition to these the following three reflections should be made: that man is by his form fitted for religious exercises, that to obtain such a body is difficult, and therefore, that he who has obtained it should give his whole attention to the subject of religion. These are the twelve spiritual reflections. Besides these there are the five sacraments. The first is, introduction to the Jain religion, *i. e.*, a vow to abstain from all injury, and to exercise compassion towards all living creatures; the second is, initiation into an ascetic life, by which all former sins are obliterated; next, the sacrament of the greater penance, [being eighteen months fasting and reading for an ascetic who threatens to leave the community]; and the lesser penance, [of shorter periods, for ebullitions of passion and slight faults]; and lastly, there is the Sacrament of Renown, when the true disciple, breaking through all the entanglements of the world, attains to the state where there is immortality and freedom from decay. There are six kinds of external austerity: entire abstinence for a limited time, taking a mouthful less and less every day; the resolution to eat only if the article, place, time, and disposition, are in accordance with a previously formed conception in the mind; the refusing all savoury articles of diet; afflicting the body, [as tearing out the hair]; restraining the senses; not looking at objects of temptation. There are also six internal austerities: repentance, humility, resolution to feed holy men, reading of holy books and instructing others in the same, religious meditation, and lastly, raising the mind above all worldly desires. Such are the restraints that prepare the mind for emancipation.

VIII. Worldly attachments. These are of four

kinds, and have reference to the nature, time, sensible qualities, and place of the objects which affect the mind. The first refers to their essence, the second to the time of their continuance, the third to their flavour, smell, &c., and the fourth to the places in which they are found. Restraints and attachments are of the following kinds: covering, [as the restraint of sight by a bandage over the eyes]; foreign agency, [as that of a porter stopping one at a door]; terror, [as the restraint from eating honey on the edge of a sharp sword]; the fascination of affection; confinement in the stocks; the attraction of beautiful objects, and paintings*; considerations of rank, [like a potter examining the different grades of the vessels he has made]; and delays, [as those experienced at the treasury when money is wanted]. So much for the subject of worldly attractions.

IX. Relative to the state of final emancipation there are six things stated: that there is really such a state, the size of the emancipated lives, and of the place where they live, their tangible qualities, the duration of their existence, the distance at which they are from one another, their parts,

* The original here is चित simply, and the explanation is "after the manner of a painter;" but I am not sure I have hit the exact idea.

their natures, their numbers. Although, however, these things may be predicated of it, nevertheless, as emancipation is a simple term, so it is expressive of a simple object, and not like sky-flower, which is a compound term embodying more than one idea. Of this thing emancipation, we are now to declare the means of attainment. The road to emancipation lies through particular states, viz., the possession of senses and a body, also the condition of possibility, or impossibility, the possession of passions, and of knowledge and vision, through the sacraments, through minute obstacles, the paths of rectitude, the possession of a mind or the contrary, and abstinence or the contrary. By these, then, emancipation is only obtained in the state of manhood, [not in that of a good demon or brute], while in possession of five senses, while possessing a body capable of voluntary motion, in a condition of possibility, while possessing a mind, through the sacrament of the highest asceticism, in that path of rectitude in which there is no retrogression, through the possession of perfect knowledge and vision, and in the practice of abstinence. It is not obtainable through any other path. The space occupied by each of the perfect is boundless, and increases according to any one's desire. The term in which they remain in this state is also infinite. Their parts are innumerable. There is no returning again to a worldly state, and no interruption to their bliss. They have perfect vision and knowledge, they have no dependence on works, but exercise themselves according to the highest philosophy. Such is the life of the Perfect.

Few neuters, [not more than ten at a time], and a small proportion of females, [not more than twenty at a time], obtain perfection; the perfect consist chiefly of males, [of which one hundred and eight may be emancipated at once]. Such is the doctrine of emancipation, and the conclusion of the Tract, or the Nine Principles of Things. He who is acquainted with these nine principles, and lays hold of them by faith, is perfect in knowledge. He who is ignorant of them cannot be perfect in knowledge. The words and doctrine of all the Jain Lords is here, and nowhere else to be found; therefore, he whose mind is instructed in these, possesses true and stable knowledge. He who has had this knowledge impressed on his mind for only an hour, is detained only by half the mental and bodily attraction that he was before.

In time there are infinite cycles, of which an infinite number have passed, and an infinite number are to come. Among sages there are the following distinctions: Jinas, and those not Jinas; Tirthankaras, and those who are not; Housholders and Mendicants, and Regular Ascetics; Men, Women, and Eunuchs; those instructed by a private individual, the self-taught, and those brought up under regular teachers; those who are emancipated singly, and those emancipated in a body.

APPENDIX.

CONTAINING REMARKS ON THE MÁGADHÍ LANGUAGE.

THE relations and affinities of the ancient and modern languages of India is a subject which has lately engaged the attention of learned Europeans. It is one, however, attended with no common difficulties. The ancient grammarian, Vararuchi, mentions not only a general Prákrit language, the relation of which to the Sanskrit he defines in several books of aphorisms, but distinguishes it also from the Suraseni, Mágadhí, and other dialects. His rules have been commented on by Colebrooke and Lassen, especially the latter; and the reader who wants information on the general subject is referred to those authorities. The following remarks have reference solely to the language in which the Kalpa Sútra, here translated, and the other ancient sacred books of the Jain community, are written; for although in comments on the ancient books, and in modern works, the Jains, as in the Introduction to the Kalpa Sútra, employ the Sanskrit, or one of the vernacular tongues, all their really ancient and standard works are written in the Mágadhí. It is a curious fact, that the Ceylonese Buddhists term their sacred tongue, usually called Pali, also Mágadhí; though on comparing the Mahávanso, one of their sacred books, with the Jain writings, I find considerable dissimilarity between the two dialects; the Pali approaching much nearer to the standard of the general Prákrit, and having few, if any, of the peculiarities of the Mágadhí dialect, while the Jain works exhibit them by no means in a slight degree. The Mahávanso probably exhibits, pretty nearly, the court language of India three hundred years before our era, when Buddhism was first firmly established in Ceylon, while the language of the Kalpa Sútra was the court language of the Balabhi monarchs of Gujarath seven centuries later; for although the two works were probably composed about the same period, the language all the while in Ceylon being a dead language, and its use confined to the priesthood, it would remain unaffected by those changes to which in India, as a spoken tongue, it would be continually subjected. In reference to the meaning of the word Prákrit, it may be observed that, among the Maráthi Brahmans, the term is often taken in its widest sense to signify the *natural* or vernacular language of any province in India. In a more restricted sense, it means any of the ancient dialects of the different provinces, and which, as most of their books used till lately to be written in it, obtains, in the south of India, the appellation Grantha. The Sanskrit is not at present a vernacular tongue, but a language polished and refined, as its name implies, for the purposes of literature; yet it seems highly probable that the ruder dialect from which the present Sanskrit has been formed was the spoken tongue of the tribe, who, under Bharat, as they themselves relate, settled in Upper India, and afterwards gave the name of their sovereign to the whole country, which extends from Cape Comorin to the Himalaya Mountains. These Bharatans then possessed, according to their own accounts, contained in the works called Puráns, and other records of their traditions, at their first emerging from obscurity, but a small portion of India, while at that time the country was peopled in every direction by tribes of a race entirely distinct, and in different stages of civilization, whom they at first denominated Daitya, Dánava, and Rákshas, and still later Mlechhas; just as till very lately, if they have even now ceased to do so, the Chinese used to call all foreigners devils, and the Greeks men of every other race, barbarians.

One of the most striking features in the institutions of those northern immigrants was the distinction of caste, which they either brought along with them, or introduced soon after their arrival in India. Yet at the first the military and priestly castes were one, and many instances can be pointed out in the Puráns where the second son of a military sovereign entered the priesthood, while his elder brother swayed the sceptre. Another striking characteristic of this tribe was, that it belonged to that grand central Asian family which has acted by far the most prominent part on the political arena of the world, sending off colonies, which became the germs of mighty monarchies in Persia, Greece, Italy, and modern Europe, as well as in India; and in all those different localities retaining the rudiments of a dialect which has formed the basis of most of those languages which contain the treasures of literature and science, as has been fully manifested by the learned labours of Schlegel, Kennedy, and Bopp. It is evident that on the spreading abroad of this northern family, and their mingling with the aborigines, a mixture of the language of the two people must have resulted. The same process, then, that took place in Spain, the north of Italy, France, and Britain, on the conquest of those countries by the Romans, took place, we must believe, in India, when the followers of Brahmanism, at different periods, took possession of its different kingdoms and principalities. The language of the aboriginal inhabitants of India, if we may judge from the Támil, that of the people most to the south, and farthest removed from Brahmanical influence, and from the dialects spoken by the hill tribes, which have never embraced the Brahmanical customs and religion, and which dialects have all much in common with the Támil, belonged to a family of languages entirely distinct from that of the northern invaders, and had a nearer resemblance to the Turkish and Siberian dialects than to any of the Indo-Germanic tongues.

It was not the policy of the Brahmans, any more than of the Romans, to dispense with the use of their own language, the record of their religion, traditions, and laws, but it required no slight modification before it could become the vernacular tongue of men whose organs of speech were utterly incapable of enunciating several of its elements, and most of its combined consonants. The old Sanskrit of the Veda, which we may suppose to have been the language of the followers of Bharat, is a harsh language compared with the musical Támil, dialects allied to which we must suppose the languages of the Indian aborigines to have been. Indeed it is admitted that the Telinga, Canarese, and other languages of the Peninsula, are closely allied to that tongue; but this is far from the whole truth; for though the languages of northern and central India borrow most of their vocables from the Brahmanical Sanskrit, yet in their grammatical construction, and the pronunciation of the letters, they more nearly resemble the Támil. Thus, for example, the letters ऋ (ṛi) and ष (sh) along with the Visarga, are unpronounceable by the great body of the population in every part of India. And as to the combinations क्ष (ksh) ष्ट (sht') क्त (kt) and a host of others, no Indian but a Brahman ever attempts to enunciate them. In regard to the inflexions of nouns in the vernacular Indian tongues, we have first the letter न (n) a very common characteristic mark of the genitive, appearing in the Támul इन (ina) the नि (ni) of the first declension in Telinga, the अन (ana) and इना (iná) of the first and fourth declensions in Canarese, the ना (ná) नि (ní)

नुं (num) of the Gujaráthi, and the चेनी (cheni) of the old Maráthi. To find anything like a parallel to this, we must pass the Sanskrit, and seek it in the Turkish ڭ In regard to the dative, the letter क (k) is the prevailing characteristic in the vernacular languages of India; thus in the Támil we have कु (ku), in the Canarese क्के (kke) of the second declension, in the Telinga कु (ku), in the Hindostani को (ko), and in the Bengali के (ke). How could there be such an analogy in respect of these the two most common and important of all the cases among languages whose vocables are so different, unless we ascribe it to the influence of an aboriginal Indian language, which obtained throughout the country, though doubtless with dialectic varieties, before the Brahmanical tongue had prevailed in nearly supplanting it everywhere, except in the Peninsula. On this, however, and on the allied subject of the affinity between the languages spoken by the mountaineers and the Támil, additional information will be found in the first volume of the "Journal of the Bombay Branch of the Royal Asiatic Society."

The Prákrit and other dialects, then, mentioned by Vararuchi had their origin in the necessity which had arisen of adapting the Brahmanical speech to the organs of the Indian aborigines, and may either be considered as corruptions or refinements, according to the standard which is used to try the qualities of languages. Having for my own part first studied the Sanskrit, and admired the accuracy with which it enables a writer to express all the varied shades of his ideas, and the niceties of its structure, I confess I felt disappointed in turning to the Prákrit; but after advancing a little in the knowledge of the language, I feel bound to concede that, by its greater simplicity of construction, and superior facility of enunciation, the Prákrit may easily bear away the palm from its rival as a simple, yet polished and harmonious vehicle of human thought, admirably fitted to be the spoken tongue of a great and refined nation; and if the reader will look back to the "explanation of Trisalá's dream," he will readily conceive that the language in which thoughts so varied and beautiful can be conveyed with ease and grace, must be something more than a jargon.

In the peculiar dialect of Prákrit termed Mágadhi, the first point mentioned by Vararuchi is the substitution of श (ś) for स (s), and ष (sh) (षसोः शः). In the common dialect, on the contrary, श (ś) and ष (sh) become स (s). Now it is a strong confirmation of this rule of the grammarian to find, that on the Ganges, whence we may suppose the model of the common Prákrit to have been taken, in all the different dialects of Hindí and Hindustaní, the स (s) is the only sibilant used, while in the Maráthi country, which anciently fell within the limits of the kingdom of Mágadha, the श (ś) is the favourite sibilant, being by the common people always substituted for स (s) before the palatine vowels इ (i) and ए (e), and the semi-vowel य (y); thus, सेवा (sevá) becomes शेवा (śevá), and सिंह (sinha) is changed to शिह (śiha). In the Gujaráthi cursive character, although both these sibilants are pronounced, the स (s) is seldom written, श (ś) being put in its place, and the proper pronunciation left to the skill of the reader.

In the Jain Mágadhí manuscripts, which are written in a form of the Nágari, varying in several letters a good deal from the Devanágari, the two letters in question seem used almost promiscuously at the pleasure of the scribe. In most of the Jain manuscripts in the Library of the Bombay Society, स (s) alone is used. In the two manuscripts of the Kalpa Sútra, from which the translation was made, श (ś) is liberally used, except in the terminations स्स (ssa) and सु su; but then the scribes seem, in the choice of one or other, to have acted quite at random, for at one time we have वसह (vasaha), and then again वशह (vaśaha) for वृषभ (vríshabha). The Yati who assisted me maintained, that the two letters should be pronounced in the same way, which, but for the authority of the grammarian, and the modern usage above referred to, I should have no solid reasons for refusing to grant. As to the proper pronunciation of the three sibilants, a Maharáshtra Brahman pronounces स (s) as the common hissing *s;* श (ś) he pronounces as a very soft *sh,* similar to these two letters in our word sheep; and ष (sh) as a very harsh *sh*, in which the tongue is raised towards the palate, as in pronouncing the ट (t') class. On the whole, I am inclined to think that श (ś) was originally more frequently written, and always pronounced by the Jains; but as far as I have had an opportunity of examining their works, any attempt now at the restoration of श (ś) to its proper place would be perfectly hopeless.

The next mark of the Mágadhí mentioned by the grammarian, is the conversion of ज (j) to य (y), the reverse of which takes place in the common Prákrit. Both changes can be instanced in our books; and as to the peculiar Mágadhí form, we have examples of it in रय (raya) for रज (raja), and गये (gaye) for गजः gaja; also in वयर (vayara) for वज्र (vajra), and राया (ráyá) for राजा (rájá); राई (raí) in Marathi, and राऊ (ráü) in Gujarathi, are more modern forms of the same word.

In the Mágadhí, the च (ch) class of letters keep their places, while in the common dialect they are elided. This answers very well as a general rule for the dialect of the Jains, but it has its exceptions, as आयरियाणं (áyariyánam) meaning आचार्येभ्यः (ácharyebhya), and probably also वयासी (vayásí) *he said;* if, as I suppose, it is from the root वच (vach). In reference to ज (j) it can only keep its place when not changed to य (y).

The change to य (y) instead of अ (a) is very common in our manuscripts, even in other cases; thus we have सेय (seya) for सेत (seta) where य (y) is used for त (t).

I have not seen the change of र्ज (rj) to य्य (yy), but the reverse, as for पर्यूषणा (paryúshana) we have पज्जउसणा (pajjausañá) according to the common Prákrit. Again भार्या (bháryyá) becomes भारिया (bháriyá) instead of the common Prákrit भारिआ (bháriä). From this word, by the application of the grammarian's rules, we shall get something nearer the Maráthi बायी (báyí) or बाई (báï).

The word ह्रदयस्य (hridayasya) has not the peculiar form with us, the grammarian mentions. Nor is र (r) changed to ल (l), except perhaps in the doubtful instances of वेरुलिय (veruliya) for वैदूर्य (vaidúrya), and उराल (urála) for उदार (udára).

I do not know how the change of क्ष (ksh) to स्क (sk) which takes place in Mágadhí, according to Vararuchi, is to be explained. In the Jain manuscripts ख (kh) is usually written रक (rak), like र (r) and क (k). Was this what the grammarian meant, and was it a mere form of writing, or is the peculiar sound intended utterly lost in the modern vernacular tongue? छ (chh) is often substituted for क्ष (ksh) as in the common dialect.

In passing, I may mention that व (v) seldom or never becomes ब (b).

In reference to one of the principal peculiarities of the Mágadhí dialect, the substitution of ए (e) for ओ (o) in the nominative singular of words, which in Sanskrit have अः (ah) or अं (am), in that case the rule of the grammarian is constantly followed in the Kalpa Sútra; thus we have गिहे (gihe) for गृहं (griham), महावीरे (mahávire) for महावीरः (mahávírah); and even in feminines in आ (á) and ई (i) the rule holds, as तिसलाए (Tisaláë) for त्रिशला (Trisalá), and माहणीए (mahaníë) for ब्राह्मणी (bráhmaní). This characteristic alone is sufficient to vindicate the correctness of the title Mágadhí, as applied to the language in which the Jain books are written; and the want of it in the Páli, shows that it has no proper claim to this peculiar epithet.

The fifth case, which should end in दु (du) or दो (do) in the writings of the Jains, as far as I have observed, always terminates simply in ऊ (ú) dropping the द (d) according to a rule which is not commonly applied to such combinations; thus we have अभंतरऊ (abhantaraü) for the Sanskrit अभ्यंतरतः (abhyantaratah). In the modern Marathi this termination becomes ऊन् (ún). There is a peculiarity also in the seventh case, the म (m) and स (s) of the Sanskrit changing places; thus we have कुच्छम्सि (kuchhamsi) and शमणम्सि (śamanamsi) while in Prákrit the termination is म्मि or म्ह

The use of the ह् (h) in the sixth case is unexampled, as far as I have observed, as well as हु (hu) in the nominative plural. The long आ (á) of the vocative is constantly used; and the Kalpa Sútra is in this point quite conformable to the rule laid down for the Mágadhí by the grammarian; thus we have always देवाणुप्पिआ (Deváñuppiä). The feminine, however, is देवाणुप्पिए (Devanuppië). The rule above mentioned holds universally in modern Márathí. The pronouns conform to the standard of the common dialect, without having any of the peculiarities mentioned by the grammarian, which probably, like some of the other things he notices, were only prevalent vulgarisms. I have not met the exceptional word छिष्टः (chhisht'a) which he mentions. The rule is the very opposite of what this word would imply; thus we have हट्ठ (hat't'ha) for हृष्ट (hrishta) and तुट्ठ (tut't'ha) for तुष्ट (tushta) as in common Prákrit.

Besides the substitution of ण (ñ) for न (n) common to all the dialects of Prákrit, Vararuchi notes the change of the other dentals to palatine letters, as a characteristic of the Mágadhí. In accordance with this rule we have निवुडे (nibuḋe) for निवृतः (nivrita) and संवुडे (Samvuḋe) for संवृतः (Samvrita) and हेड (heḋa) for हतः (hata). This also is one of the striking peculiarities of the modern Márathí language, as compared with the other vernacular dialects of India; thus we have गांठ (gánth) for ग्रंथि (granthi) and वाणी (báṅí) for ध्वनि (dhwani) and डंख (ḋankha) for दंश (danśa) and डंभ (ḋambha) for दंभ (dambha) and a hundred others, in the common vernacular dialects.

The peculiar preter-past participle in दाणि (dáṅi) has not fallen under my observation. There are two forms of this participle in common use, one in ट्टु (t′t′u) as कट्टु (kat′t′u) and the other in इत्ता (ittá) as करित्ता (karittá) both meaning कृत्वा (kritvá). The nearest to दाणि (dáṅi) is the form इताणं (itánam) which occurs not unfrequently as in the word पाशिताणं (páśitaṅam) used for पाशित्ता (paśittá) from the root पश (paśa) in the sense of दृष्ट्वा (drisht́vá).

In the third person singular present indicative of the verb, the contracted form करेइ (kareï) is always used, contrary to the Páli practice, which mostly keeps the त (t) of the Sanskrit in the termination, while the Prákrit substitutes generally द (d).

Enough, then, has been said to show that the Jain books are not written entirely in the peculiar Mágadhí of Vararuchi. The language will correspond more nearly to his Ardhamágadhika, though not to that entirely either. It is a pecular dialect, having a decidedly Mágadhí leaning, but differing in several respects from all the specimens of Prákrit found in the Hindu dramatic works, from which the grammarian's rules seem originally to have been been derived. Probably a closer and more critical study of the Jain works in their relation to the Sanskrit, Prákrit, Páli, and other dialects, might bring to light other points of difference; but these remarks, it is hoped, will give the reader a tolerably correct notion of the general character of the language of the original works from which the foregoing translations were made. I must observe, however, that there are differences in these works themselves, and that my remarks in this Appendix have almost sole reference to the language of the Kalpa Sútra, the other tract approaching much nearer to the common Prákrit, and the untranslated manuscripts in the Library having been only occasionally consulted.